Strategic Implications of Hybrid War: A Theory of Victory

Daniel T. Lasica

This is a curated and comprehensive collection of the most important works covering matters related to national security, diplomacy, defense, war, strategy, and tactics. The collection spans centuries of thought and experience, and includes the latest analysis of international threats, both conventional and asymmetric. It also includes riveting first person accounts of historic battles and wars.

Some of the books in this Series are reproductions of historical works preserved by some of the leading libraries in the world. As with any reproduction of a historical artifact, some of these books contain missing or blurred pages, poor pictures, errant marks, etc. We believe these books are essential to this collection and the study of war, and have therefore brought them back into print, despite these imperfections.

We hope you enjoy the unmatched breadth and depth of this collection, from the historical to the just-published works.

Strategic Implications of Hybrid War: A Theory of Victory

A Monograph
by
Lt Col Daniel T. Lasica
United States Air Force

School of Advanced Military Studies
United States Army Command and General Staff College
Fort Leavenworth, Kansas

AY 2009

REPORT DOCUMENTATION PAGE

1. REPORT DATE *(DD-MM-YYYY)*	2. REPORT TYPE	3. DATES COVERED *(From - To)*
30-04-2009	MONOGRAPH	July 2008 - May 2009

4. TITLE AND SUBTITLE	
Strategic Implications of Hybrid War: A Theory of Victory	5a. CONTRACT NUMBER
	5c. PROGRAM ELEMENT NUMBER

6. AUTHOR(S)	
	5d. PROJECT NUMBER
Lt Col Daniel T. Lasica, USAF	5e. TASK NUMBER
	5f. WORK UNIT NUMBER

7. PERFORMING ORGANIZATION NAME(S) AND ADDRESS(ES)	8. PERFORMING ORGANIZATION REPORT NUMBER
Advanced Military Studies Program 250 Gibbon Ave Fort Leavenworth, KS 66027-2134	CGSC, SAMS

9. SPONSORING/MONITORING AGENCY NAME(S) AND ADDRESS(ES)	10. SPONSOR/MONITOR'S ACRONYM(S)
Command and General Staff College 1 Reynolds Ave Fort Leavenworth, KS 66027	
	11. SPONSOR/MONITOR'S REPORT NUM

12. DISTRIBUTION / AVAILABILITY STATEMENT

Approved for Public Release; Distribution is Unlimited

13. SUPPLEMENTARY:

ABSTRACT

While the nature of war does not change, the conduct and methods available to wage and win wars does. This appears to be the case with respect to hybrid war, an evolving type of war that the United States may soon face. The definition of hybrid war is the merging of different methods and theories of war and warfare at different levels of war, in different realms and domains, especially the cognitive and moral domains, by a blend of actors, arranged in time and space to achieve objectives at all levels of war. Hybrid war poses a novel threat to the United States for many reasons, including undue U.S. attention on irregular warfare as the "war of the future," as well as hybrid war's blending of modes at different levels of war using different theories of war and warfare.

Recent discussions about hybrid war have been primarily focused at the tactical and to a lesser degree at the operational level, not at the strategic level where hybrid war should also be considered. A vital part of "strategic art" is developing a theory of victory. This paper's thesis is that the United States needs to develop a hybrid war theory of victory, which is combining "how to win the war" and "what is winning." Generic principles of "what is winning" will be used as criteria to develop a theory of war relevant to the hybrid warrior. This theory will help enable the United States to determine if and how national power should be used in a hybrid war to achieve strategic political objectives and what the probable outcomes of military conflict might be in that situation. This, in turn, will help senior decision makers determine the best ways to achieve strategic objectives and protect national interests.

One of the biggest challenges hybrid war presents is exploitation of the cognitive and moral domains, vice the physical domain that the United States traditionally concentrates on. The United States may consider giving the cognitive and moral domain more emphasis in its approaches to resolving the complex problems that hybrid war presents. This, as well as a joint, inter-agency approach will allow the United States to meet complexity with complexity and attain victory. Using an approach that concentrates on identity and meaning may also be beneficial in understanding the hybrid rival and framing a theory of victory. The value of developing a theory of victory to address hybrid war, a significant threat, cannot be overstated.

SUBJECT TERMS

Theory of Victory, Hybrid War, Strategy, Levels of War, Complexity, Domains of War, Problem Resolution, Theories of War and Warfare

SECURITY CLASSIFICATION OF:			17. LIMITATION OF ABSTRACT	18. NUMBER OF PAGES	19a. NAME OF RESPONSIBLE PERSON Stefan J. Banach, COL, U.S. Army
REPORT UNCLASSIFIED	b. ABSTRACT UNCLASSIFIED	c. THIS PAGE UNCLASSIFIED	UNLIMITED	48	19b. TELEPHONE NUMBER *(include area code)* 913-758-3302

Standard Form 298 (Rev. 8-98)

SCHOOL OF ADVANCED MILITARY STUDIES

MONOGRAPH APPROVAL

Lt Col Daniel Todd Lasica

Title of Monograph: Strategic Implications of Hybrid War: A Theory of Victory

Approved by:

_____   Monograph Director
Richard D. Newton, Lt Col (R), USAF, MMAS

_____   Director,
Stefan Banach, COL, IN   School of Advanced
                                         Military Studies

_____   Director,
Robert F. Baumann, Ph.D.   Graduate Degree
                                         Programs

Abstract

STRATEGIC IMPLICATIONS OF HYBRID WAR: A THEORY OF VICTORY by Lt Col
Daniel T. Lasica, United States Air Force, 48.

While the nature of war does not change, the conduct and methods available to wage and
win wars does. This appears to be the case with respect to hybrid war, an evolving type of war
that the United States may soon face. The definition of hybrid war is the merging of different
methods and theories of war and warfare at different levels of war, in different realms and
domains, especially the cognitive and moral domains, by a blend of actors, arranged in time and
space to achieve objectives at all levels of war. Hybrid war poses a novel threat to the United
States for many reasons, including undue U.S. attention on irregular warfare as the "war of the
future," as well as hybrid war's blending of modes at different levels of war using different
theories of war and warfare.

Recent discussions about hybrid war have been primarily focused at the tactical and to a
lesser degree at the operational level, not at the strategic level where hybrid war should also be
considered. A vital part of "strategic art" is developing a theory of victory. This paper's thesis is
that the United States needs to develop a hybrid war theory of victory, which is combining "how
to win the war" and "what is winning." Generic principles of "what is winning" will be used as
criteria to develop a theory of war relevant to the hybrid warrior. This theory will help enable the
United States to determine if and how national power should be used in a hybrid war to achieve
strategic political objectives and what the probable outcomes of military conflict might be in that
situation. This, in turn, will help senior decision makers determine the best ways to achieve
strategic objectives and protect national interests.

One of the biggest challenges hybrid war presents is exploitation of the cognitive and
moral domains, vice the physical domain that the United States traditionally concentrates on. The
United States may consider giving the cognitive and moral domain more emphasis in its
approaches to resolving the complex problems that hybrid war presents. This, as well as a joint,
inter-agency approach will allow the United States to meet complexity with complexity and attain
victory. Using an approach that concentrates on identity and meaning may also be beneficial in
understanding the hybrid rival and framing a theory of victory. The value of developing a theory
of victory to address hybrid war, a significant threat, cannot be overstated.

TABLE OF CONTENTS

The true national objective in war, as in peace, is a more perfect peace. The experience of history enables us to deduce that gaining military victory is not in itself equivalent to gaining the object of war.

- Captain Sir Basil Liddell Hart, Thoughts on War, 1944

Introduction

Consider this scenario looking forward to the year 2011. The world community has confirmed that Iran has developed nuclear weapons technology. Emboldened by this new capability, they have sought to become a regional hegemon. Saudi Arabia, feeling threatened, announces its intention to acquire nuclear weapons of its own. In response, Iran, with the help of Hezbollah, attacks Saudi Arabia using conventional and irregular means in multiple domains.[1] Surface to surface missiles rain down on Saudi Arabia.

Simultaneously, Iran attacks much of the Saudi oil infrastructure causing an environmental disaster. They also close the Strait of Hormuz, choking off one of the Saudi's main economic lifelines, in addition to attacking the Saudi's computer infrastructure with intense cyber attacks. Iran also calls for the nuclear destruction of the United States and Israel, blaming Saudi

---

[1] 20th century British military theorist J.F.C. Fuller developed a framework to study war that included three spheres (domains), physical, mental (cognitive), and moral. The physical domain includes the material used to fight wars, such as tanks, ships, and aircraft and how they are used; moving, guarding, and hitting. The cognitive domain includes reason, imagination, and will. In the context of this paper, the cognitive domain is "where" the intellectual rigor is expended, ideas developed, and decisions made to defeat the enemy. This effort includes such activities as designing campaigns and planning major operations "to win" and developing an idea of "what winning is." The moral domain is much more subjective since it deals with many intangibles of war. It includes fear, courage, and the morale of all parties involved in the conflict. J.F.C.Fuller, *The Foundations of the Science of War* (London: Hutchinson & Co., Ltd., 1925). Fuller also discusses the concept of will a great deal in his discussion of the moral sphere. For the purposes of this paper, "will" will "reside" in the moral domain. This a more contemporary understanding of the moral domain, as described by School of Advanced Military Studies professor James Schneider. James Schneider, "Carl von Clausewitz and the Classical Military Paradigm," Briefing given to the School of Advanced Military Studies, Fort Leavenworth, KS, September 22, 2006, 2. Additionally, Clausewitz addresses similar concepts. Clausewitz discusses moral factors and elements, which he states, "are among the most important in war." Carl von Clausewitz, *On War,* ed. Michael Howard and Peter Paret. (Princeton: Princeton University Press, 1976), 184. He also discusses such elements of the physical domain such as forces, logistics, and firepower. Carl von Clausewitz, 204-209. Additionally, Clausewitz addresses the cognitive domain in many parts of his book, including his discussion of military genius and war plans. Carl von Clausewitz, 100 and 617. In fact, Clausewitz maintains that, "Genius consists in a harmonious combination of elements." Carl von Clausewitz, 100.

Arabia's betrayal to the Muslim cause on the United States. Hezbollah, at Iran's request, initiates anti-Israeli demonstrations in major Palestinian cities and instigates a boycott of Israeli owned businesses. An intense information operations campaign ensues, seeking to gather Muslim support against Saudi Arabia, "lapdog" of the United States, as well as to convince the American public that Saudi Arabia is not worth its blood and treasure. The grave threat to itself and two of its key allies compels the United States to take action.

Once battle is joined, it is evident that this enemy is well equipped and ready to challenge the United States. Iran simultaneously uses a blend of conventional and irregular methods of warfare with a robust strategic communication and information operations campaign. Included in their information operations campaign are "strikes" against U.S. military and civilian computer networks.

Iran initiates temporally coordinated attacks against the United States in all three different domains; physical, moral, and cognitive, clearly indicating a very sophisticated enemy that intends to attack any and all perceived U.S. vulnerabilities. The battle in the cognitive and moral domains is especially intense. The enemy seeks to gain regional, if not international, legitimacy in its fight against the United States and they target U.S. public will, a known critical vulnerability.

This fictional, albeit not unrealistic, scenario is an example of an evolving hybrid war challenge to vital U.S. interests.[2] While the nature of war does not change, the conduct and methods available to wage and win wars does. This appears to be the case with respect to hybrid war. As described by the United States Marine Corps Strategic Vision Group, "Hybrid Wars combine a range of different modes of warfare, including conventional capabilities, irregular tactics and formations, terrorist acts including indiscriminate violence and coercion, and criminal

---

[2] Of note, this type of threat is not isolated to the Middle East. As an example, China is a very credible hybrid threat whose economic and military might are on the rise.

disorder."[3] This paper will take a broader approach to hybrid war, defining it as the merging of different methods and theories of war at different levels of war, in different realms and domains, especially the cognitive and moral domains, by a blend of actors, arranged in time and space to achieve objectives at all levels of war.

The hybrid warrior seeks to quickly convert their tactical success and their enemy's mistakes into strategic effects through deliberate exploitation of the cognitive and moral domains. Hybrid war is a strategy and a tactic, a form of war and warfare. Hybrid warriors seek to compress the U.S.' concept of the levels of war, thus accelerating the tempo of the conduct of war. As strategic scholar Colin Gray has noted, "we can predict with confidence is that there is going to be a blurring, a further blurring, of war categories."[4]

The hybrid war threat is beginning to gain interest in security communities around the world, including the United States, Britain, and Australia. Australian Michael Evans stated that, "the reality of war in the first decade of the twenty-first century is likely to transcend a neat division into distinct categories, symmetry and asymmetry."[5]

Recent discussions about hybrid war have been primarily focused at the tactical and to a lesser degree at the operational level, not at the strategic level where hybrid war should also be considered. Colin Gray once asked, "Who, exactly, peoples the profession of strategy?"[6] Of those

---

[3] U.S. Marine Corps, "Hybrid Warfare and Challengers" (Strategic Vision Group Information Paper, February 12, 2008), 1.

[4] Colin S. Gray, *Another Bloody Century: Future Warfare* (London: Weidenfeld and Nicholson, 2005), quoted in U.S. Marine Corps, "Hybrid Warfare and Challengers" (Strategic Vision Group Information Paper, February 12, 2008), 1.

[5] Michael Evans, "From Kadesh to Kandahar: Military Theory and the Future of War," *Naval War College Review 56*, no. 3 (Summer 2003): 141.

[6] Colin S. Gray, *Modern Strategy,* (Oxford: Oxford University Press, 1999), quoted in Michael Evans, "From the Long Peace to the Long War: Armed Conflict and Military Education and Training in the 21st Century," *Australian Defence College Occasional Series*, no. 1 (2007): 14.

who are thinking strategically, how many are considering hybrid war and how this threat affects the concept of the U.S. theory of victory?

A theory of victory is a cognitive theoretical framework within which senior decision makers determine the most effective and efficient manner to, as author Brian Bonds describes, achieve a decisive military victory and turn it into positive political gains.[7] In his book, *The Pursuit of Victory,* Brian Bond illustrates two related problems warring parties have faced from the mid-eighteenth century to the present with respect to victory.[8] The first is the operational difficulties involved in winning decisive campaign victories. The second, and often ill coordinated with the first, is the translation of those victories into long-term political advantages.[9] This paper will define theory of victory as the sum of "how to win wars" and the understanding of "what is winning" at the strategic level.[10] Seen another way, it is the convergence of "Ways" and "Ends." Both these aspects are unique in the context of the hybrid war challenge and will be investigated in this paper to define a U.S. theory of victory with respect to hybrid war.

Developing a theory of victory with regard to hybrid war is necessary because instead of investigating the hybrid war threat, especially with respect to a theory of victory, it is very possible that the United States focuses too much on irregular warfare as the type of war it will most likely face in the future.[11] Irregular warfare capability should be "A" U.S. capability, not "THE" capability the United States prepares for at all three levels of war.

---

[7] J. Boone Bartholomees, "Theory of Victory," *Parameters* (Summer 2008): 25 and Brian Bond, *The Pursuit of Victory: From Napoleon to Saddam Hussein* (New York: Oxford University Press, 1996), 201-202.

[8] Brian Bond, 201-202.

[9] Ibid.

[10] J. Boone Bartholomees, 25.

[11] This paper will use the Department of Defense definition of irregular warfare, "A violent struggle among state and non-state actors for legitimacy and influence over the relevant populations. IW favors indirect and asymmetric approaches, though it may employ the full range of military and other

After overthrow of the respective regimes, the United States initially had considerable difficulty fighting an irregular campaign in Iraq and now in Afghanistan. The insurgents posed a threat the United States was not ready for and did not initially recognize. In *On War*, Clausewitz states that the first and arguably most important duty of a commander and statesman is to understand the type of the war they face.[12] In order to understand the war that faces them, the commander and statesman must first recognize it for what it is or they may face dangerous consequences.

These consequences partially arise from the potential effects of a threat blending into a concerted cyber, space, irregular, conventional, economic, criminal, or nuclear threat. Hezbollah vividly demonstrated the effectiveness of a hybrid challenger in 2006 against Israel and it is very probable that adversaries could use such a form of hybrid war against the United States in the near future. This form of war exists as a potential model that future adversaries could use.

It is logical then, to investigate the threat that a hybrid war challenger might pose to the United States in terms of one of the 2008 National Defense Strategy (NDS) five key objectives, Win Our Nation's Wars.[13] U.S. strategic planning tends to neatly categorize threats instead of understanding the blending of threats that could exist, characterizing threats as either conventional *or* irregular. The 2008 NDS describes adversaries that, "could be states *or* [emphasis added] non-state actors; they could use nuclear, conventional, *or* [emphasis added] unconventional weapons."[14] This mindset could lead to an inability on the part of the United States to develop a theory of victory for and execute against, a "future challenges risk" as outlined

---

capabilities, in order to erode an adversary's power, influence, and will." U.S. Department of Defense, *Irregular Warfare (IW) Joint Operating Concept (JOC)*, Version 1.0, September 11, 2007, 6.

[12] Carl von Clausewitz, 88-89.

[13] U.S. Department of Defense, *National Defense Strategy*, June 2008, 6. There is another of the five key objectives that is relevant in relation to the hybrid war threat, "Deter Conflict." This key objective is an additional topic recommended for further study with respect to hybrid war.

[14] U.S. Department of Defense, *National Defense Strategy*, 11.

in the 2008 NDS. These risks are "those associated with the Department's capacity to execute future missions successfully against an array of prospective future challengers," such as a hybrid challenger.[15] As noted by General James Mattis, USMC, Joint Forces Command commander, "We are not likely to get the future right. We just need to make sure we don't get it too wrong."[16]

As an example, aspects of a hybrid challenger were evident during Russia's struggle against Chechnya in the 1990s. Chechnyan fighters fought both conventionally and unconventionally in the same battlespace and used complex urban terrain, modern weapons, and robust information operations to repel the Russians.[17] In 2006, Hezbollah battled the Israeli Defense Forces using a blend of conventional, irregular, and information methods of warfare.[18] This was a more advanced use of hybrid war than the Chechnyan separatists used against Russia due to the more advanced weapons available and the intense battle Hezbollah fought in the cognitive and moral domains to quickly achieve strategic effects using the results of tactical battles.[19] The determination of undisputed victory in that war is still unresolved.[20]

---

[15] U.S. Department of Defense, *National Defense Strategy,* 21.

[16] James Mattis, USMC, quoted in Mackubin Thomas Owens, "Reflections on Future War," *Naval War College Review 61* (Summer 2008): 74.

[17] "Grisly in Grozny," *Economist,* January 7, 1995 and Sergey A. Kulikov and Robert R. Love, "Insurgent Groups in Chechnya," *Military Review* (Nov/Dec 2003).

[18] William M. Arkin. *Divining Victory: Airpower in the 2006 Israel-Hezbollah War* (Maxwell AFB, AL: Air University Press, August 2007), xix. The Israeli-Hezbollah War of 2006 also illustrates some of the difficulties a nation can face when it concentrates too much on one type of warfare. In the case of the Israeli's, they concentrated too heavily on counterinsurgency. Due to years of concentrating on the internal threat presented by the Palestinian Liberation Organization and Hamas, the Israeli Defense Force had let its conventional warfighting capabilities lapse. Matt M. Mathews, "We Were Caught Unprepared: The 2006 Hezbollah-Israeli War," *The Long War Series Occasional Paper 26.* U.S. Army Combined Arms Center Combat Studies Institute Press, 2. This was just one of many factors that led to what many consider a strategic defeat for Israel.

[19] Sarah E. Kreps, "The 2006 Lebanon War: Lessons Learned," *Parameters* (Spring 2007): 79-80.

[20] Retired Lebanese Brigadier General Hanna noted of Hezbollah during Hezbollah's 2006 war with Israel that it may be impossible to truly judge victory with actors like Hezbollah. Brigadier General Hanna also holds that Israel achieved no political goals. Elias Hanna, "Lessons Learned from the Recent War in Lebanon," *Military Review* (September-October 2007): 89 and 86.

Russia's 2008 invasion of Georgia demonstrated even wider, yet shallower aspects of hybrid war since the invasion displayed a heavier concentration of conventional warfare and seemingly less battle in the cognitive and moral domains. However, the Russian attempts at modest information, cyber, and economic warfare were significant.[21] What will the next hybrid war evolution look like and will it target the United States? Are we ready? Clearly, hybrid war seems to be evolving and will eventually pose a threat to the United States.

As the current wars in Afghanistan and Iraq illustrate, the ability to develop a theory of victory before and adjusting it during a conflict is paramount. Not developing a theory of victory raises the possibility of catastrophic strategic consequences. The Vietnam War offers an example of the outcome of not having a sound theory of victory, among other problems. Had the U.S. strategic leadership considered a theory of victory, they may not have entered that conflict. However, if the leadership thought the war was necessary, a theory of victory, defining "how to win" plus determining "what is victory", may have led to a more favorable outcome for the United States.

This paper's thesis is that the United States needs to frame a hybrid war theory of victory, which combines "how to win" and "what is winning." This framework is different than other theories of victory because it describes a theory of victory in the context of hybrid war. This theory will help determine if and how a senior leader should use national power in a hybrid war environment to achieve strategic political objectives and what the probable outcomes of military

---

[21] The Russian-Georgian scenario of 2008 is an example of a Western nation state attempting to use aspects of hybrid war. It is evidenced by heavy use of conventional forces in the physical domain and less emphasis on the cognitive domain. Clearly, to achieve their strategic objectives, the Russians did not need to resort to true hybrid war because of their preponderance of conventional military might against a small conventional threat. The previous two examples, the Chechnyans and Hezbollah, illustrate a more pure hybrid threat against a superior equipped western nation state. This was especially true in the battle for the cognitive and moral domains, which Hezbollah was compelled to resort to because of an inferior military. Siobhan Gorman, "Georgia States' Computers Hit By Cyberattack," *Wall Street Journal,* August 12, 2008. Thom Shanker, "Russians Blend Old-School Blitz with Modern Military Tactics," *New York Times,* August 17, 2008.

conflict might be in that situation. This, in turn, will help senior decision makers determine the best "Ways" to achieve strategic objectives and protect national interests.

In order to fully explore hybrid war and an applicable theory of victory, the definitions of war and warfare will be considered. This discussion will lead to an examination of several theories of war and warfare. The concept of hybrid war as a hybrid of war and warfare theories will also be considered. Theory of victory will then be discussed and its significance examined with an emphasis on the challenge hybrid war poses to achieving decisive victory and the ability to convert military successes into long-term political gains. Next, the first part of the theory of victory equation, "How to win" at the strategic level, will be examined. A general discussion of the more difficult second half of the equation, "what is winning" at the strategic level will follow. These principles will then be used as criteria to compare and contrast the concept of "what is winning" in a hybrid war environment. The paper will conclude with a summarization of the analysis conducted. Finally, recommendations will then be made as to a way ahead for the United States' theory of victory with respect to hybrid war.

Literature Review

To understand hybrid war, it is useful to deconstruct the words "hybrid", "war", and "warfare." This will lay a theoretical foundation by drawing boundaries for these terms. According to The American Heritage Dictionary, "hybrid" is "something of mixed origin or composition."[22] With respect to hybrid war, some see this "mixing" simply as a blurring of capabilities at the tactical level, such as a Hezbollah guerilla fighter using a high-tech anti-tank weapon.[23] This tactical example is only a very small portion of the hybrid aspect of these

---

[22] The American Heritage Dictionary, Second College Edition, (Boston: Houghton Mifflin Company, 1985), 629.

[23] Matthew Rusling, "Shifting Gears: For the Military, a Future of 'hybrid' wars," *National Defense,* (September 2008): 32.

challenges, but it tends to be the one many analysts and scholars focus on. What is more important to examine is different modes of warfare combined to achieve strategic effects and increase the complexity of the situation.

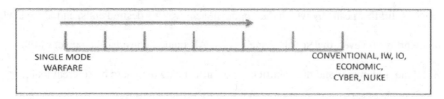

Figure 1. Hybrid War Complexity Continuum

Understanding the terms "war" and "warfare" are critical when considering hybrid war. The concept of war will be examined first. According to Clausewitz, "War is thus an act of force to compel our enemy to do our will."[24] As Colin Gray maintains, the nature of war never changes.[25] Gray also describes war as a relationship between belligerents, "employed and misemployed by flawed people for a host of reasons."[26] He also depicts, as does Clausewitz, war as primarily political, since violence without political content is crime.[27] Thus, victory, the purpose of war, is pursued for political objectives.[28]

One scholar who disagrees with the concept that the nature of war is constant, Dr. John Alexander, suggests that information technology enhances the ability of entities (state, non-state, criminal) to impose their will on an adversary. He holds that it is the ability of a belligerent to impose its will, not the amount of violence achieved, that will decide the winner of any given

---

[24] Carl von Clausewitz, 75.

[25] Colin S. Gray, *Another Bloody Century: Future Warfare*, 30.

[26] Colin S. Gray, "Defining and Achieving Decisive Victory," (U.S. Army War College Strategic Studies Institute Monograph, Carlisle Barracks, PA, April 2002), 7.

[27] Colin S. Gray, *Another Bloody Century: Future Warfare*, 30.

[28] Colin S. Gray, *War, Peace, and International Relations: An Introduction to Strategic History.* (New York: Routledge, 2007), 8.

conflict.[29] Alexander, then, asks the fundamental question of whether or not violence remains a necessary component of war. This author maintains that violence absolutely remains a necessary component of war, but understands that it does not hold a monopoly in war and warfare as it once did. Violence is still the means by which the opponent achieves his desired ends, and always will be. It is noteworthy however, that scholars such as Dr. Alexander, consider the power of the cognitive and moral domains and the significance of influencing people to be so great that it is changing the very nature of war.

War is a broad concept that includes the concept of warfare, in addition to strategy, justification for going to war, theories of victory, and sustainment of the war effort, to name just a few. War, therefore, can be considered a strategic concept.

Warfare, however, can be considered a tactical concept whose character changes with time, as Gray maintains.[30] Mackubin Owens, Naval War College professor, describes this changing character as infinite, allowing weaker adversaries to use different types of warfare to confront and possibly defeat stronger opponents.[31] Examples of the different types of warfare include conventional, irregular, information, cyber, nuclear, and economic.

The hybrid warrior attempts to simultaneously blend these types of warfare in different domains, simultaneously, in the battlespace. Their goal is to accelerate the tempo of warfare while achieving strategic effects. Lest one disregard the hybrid war threat and think a weaker enemy cannot defeat the United States, weaker belligerents have been successful against stronger opponents approximately 40 percent of the time since World War II.[32]

---

[29] John B. Alexander, "The Changing Nature of War, the Factors Mediating Future Conflict, and Implications for SOF," (Joint Special Operations University Report 06-1, Hurlburt Field, FL, April 2006), 1.

[30] Colin S. Gray, *Another Bloody Century: Future Warfare*, 32.

[31] Mackubin Thomas Owens, 67.

[32] Ibid.

Synthesizing the terms hybrid and war then, hybrid war is a combination of strategy and tactics designed to mix the types of warfare to use tactical success to achieve strategic effects by quickly exploiting the cognitive and moral domains. Hybrid war is not only hybrid in its capabilities and its effects, but more important to understanding and combating it is that hybrid war is hybrid in its theory and logic as well. Aspects of classical theorists such as Clausewitz and Sun Tzu, as well as newer theorists like Mao, and proponents of Unrestricted Warfare and Fourth Generation Warfare can be used to describe hybrid war. This presents a difficult challenge for the United States as a fusion of the most appropriate aspects of these different theories challenge U.S. vulnerabilities.

First, threats attempting to generate a hybrid war environment seem to understand Clausewitz's concept of a belligerent's power of resistance being the product of means and will.[33] As the world's only superpower, the United States' military and economic means are unmatched. Threats attempting to generate a hybrid war environment understand this and thus seek to challenge the United States with modest military means in an asymmetric manner, while focusing on the U.S. will to fight. The ultimate aim of threats in a hybrid war is to directly target the U.S. will to fight using a variety of modes of warfare. There is a large conceptual difference between this mindset and the U.S. mindset that seeks an indirect approach to an opponent's will through its armed forces.

Hybrid war threats also seem to understand Clausewitz's center of gravity concept, especially as it relates to the U.S.' will to fight. They realize that the public is the U.S. center of gravity, with the will to fight being a critical vulnerability. Globalization has presented many opportunities to exploit this vulnerability, especially in the economic and informational realms. The prolonged wars in Iraq and Afghanistan have tapped a great deal of critical human and

---

[33] Carl von Clausewitz, 77.

material resources and have strained the U.S. will to fight, making the United States even more vulnerable to a future hybrid war threat. Astute hybrid war adversaries could exploit this vulnerability in the future by attacking in the cognitive and moral domains.

Actions taken by hybrid warriors also exhibit several of Sun Tzu's concepts. They subscribe to the oft-quoted Sun Tzu adage to know thyself and thy enemy and in a hundred battles you will never be endangered.[34] On many different levels, it seems these challengers know the U.S. much better than we know ourselves. It is also true that they know us better than we know them. As Sun Tzu maintains, this aids the ability of adversaries (in a hybrid war) to manipulate U.S. psychology.[35] It also allows a belligerent to act beyond their enemy's understanding, a key point when attacking in the cognitive domain.[36]

Another important aspect of Sun Tzu's teachings evident in a hybrid war is the importance of changing form, appropriately adapting to conflict situations by the employment of different types and size of forces.[37] Sun Tzu espouses the use of both regular and irregular actions to defeat the enemy. Sun Tzu also suggests weakening the enemy through both asymmetric and unconventional means that exploit weaknesses by targeting vulnerabilities, all key pillars of the hybrid war approach.[38] Fluidity and flexibility, not only of forces, but of strategy, also appear to be key aspects of Sun Tzu's teachings that emerge in hybrid war.[39]

---

[34] Sun Tzu, *The Art of War.* trans. Samuel B. Griffith (New York: Oxford University Press, 1963), 129.

[35] Sun Tzu, *The Art of War.* trans. J.H. Huang, (New York: Quill, William Morrow Publishers, 1993), 62.

[36] Ibid., 63.

[37] Ibid., 68.

[38] Ibid., 58.

[39] Ibid., 67-68.

Sun Tzu's theories heavily influenced Mao Zedong, so it holds that aspects of Mao Zedong's teachings may influence hybrid warriors. His ideas may appeal to a hybrid threat because a weak agent in the system can defeat a more powerful opponent by combining asymmetrical types of warfare with a strategy designed to influence an audience in the cognitive and moral domains.[40] Mao's ideas are different than hybrid war concepts, however, in that hybrid war challenges a state externally. Significantly, Mao Zedong also wrote that a decisive military battle does not exist in this type of war.[41] Mao's concept of victory, similar to a hybrid warrior's concept, is a political victory. These ideas fundamentally contradict the current American concept of a military focused theory of victory.

There are also many relevant ideas from the Unrestricted Warfare school of thought an adversary has the potential to apply while attempting to generate hybrid war. The Chinese authors hold that there is a revolution in military thought that transcends technological revolutions.[42] An example of this thought is the hybrid warrior's fusion of strategy and tactics, as well as the mixed fighting forms and methods that are influenced by a logic similar to Sun Tzu and Mao. These concepts are problematic for the United States because it often aspires to action and technological answers to problems vice searching for cognitive solutions that exploit the propensity of a system

---

[40] Thomas A. Marks, "Insurgency in Nepal," *Strategic Studies Institute,* U.S. Army War College, December 2003, 6-7.

[41] Mao, Zedong. *On Guerilla War.* 1937. http://www.marxists.org/reference/archive/mao/works/1937/guerrilla-war/, Ch 2, page 1. (accessed January 29, 2009).

[42] Liang and Xiangsu also describe a mixed conduct of warfare through three indispensible "hardware" elements of warfare, soldiers, weapons, and the battlefield, that couple with the "software" of purposefulness. These elements, akin to Clausewitz's means and will, are changing in the current globalized world and increasingly threaten U.S. vulnerabilities. Adversaries are increasingly likely to not only use military power, but also use information technologies, cyber attacks and trade disruptions to target the U.S.' potential weaknesses caused by an economy and society that has become intertwined with the rest of the world. Qiao Liang and Wang Xiangsui, *Unrestricted Warfare: China's Master Plan to Destroy America* Panama City: Pan American Publishing Co., 2002), 94 and 25.

to solve a problem. Eastern schools of thought are antithetical to Western concepts in many ways, as the different approaches to war identified by Clausewitz and Sun Tzu illustrate.[43]

Lastly, there are aspects of the much-debated Fourth Generation Warfare theory that are useful in describing and explaining certain aspects of the hybrid war threat. In fact, al Qaeda has discussed Fourth Generation Warfare on one of its websites, stating it uses some Fourth Generation Warfare concepts.[44] A Fourth Generation opponent will most likely be barbaric and fight to the death, often motivated by radical ideology. They will also use networks, as Hezbollah did in 2006, possibly linking state, non-state, and criminal organizations. Additionally, Fourth Generation Warfare, like hybrid war, stresses the importance of the use of the cognitive domain in influencing different agents in the system.

There are large differences between adversaries operating in a hybrid war environment and a Fourth Generation warrior, however.[45] Once again, very similar to Mao, Fourth Generation Warfare focuses exclusively on internal threats or irregular threats, as categorized by U.S. doctrine. Fourth Generation Warfare comprises just a portion of the much broader hybrid war spectrum of capabilities and implications.[46]

---

[43] Francois Jullien, *A Treatise of Efficacy* (Honolulu: University of Hawaii Press, 2004), vii-viii.

[44] T.X. Hammes, "Fourth Generation Warfare Evolves, Fifth Emerges," *Military Review* (May-June 2007), 14.

[45] Thomas X. Hammes, *The Sling and the Stone: On War in the 21st Century* (St. Paul: Zenith Press, 2006), 2. Fourth generation warfare (4GW), as defined by Col Hammes is an evolved form of insurgency when an adversary uses all available networks, political, economic, social, and military, to target the enemy's decision makers that their objectives are either unattainable or too costly. While there are elements of 4GW in hybrid war, hybrid war is a much broader concept that focuses on external threats vice the internal threats 4GW describes.

[46] Significantly, many dispute the idea that Fourth Generation warfare is actually a theory. Additionally, although it does have some merit (as discussed above), the fact that Fourth Generation Warfare theory is being considered so rigorously is evidence that many in this country are focused on too narrow of a threat. Too narrow of a focus can have negative strategic implications in the future.

Hybrid war is not a description of the next Afghanistan or Iraq. Hybrid war is a departure from the current strategic paradigm that seems mired in counterinsurgency. This counterinsurgency focus naturally stems from the two most recent and still ongoing conflicts the United States is involved in that were initiated by the United States' perceived need for regime change in Iraq and Afghanistan. Regime change will not be the primary political objective for every war the United States will fight in the future. Additionally, every regime change will not result in an insurgency.

Just as with the concept of hybrid war, it is useful to deconstruct the concept of the theory of victory. J. Boone Bartholomees, U.S. Army War College professor, describes the theory of victory as "the biggest theoretical challenge facing security professionals today."[47] To begin the discussion, a useful definition of victory is, "a successful struggle against an opponent or obstacle."[48]

A theory of victory is a cognitive theoretical framework within which senior decision makers determine the most effective and efficient manner to gain a decisive military victory and turn it into lasting, positive political gains.[49] Colin Gray describes it in the form of strategic advantages and successes where different degrees are acceptable, while J. Boone Bartholomees uses scales to describe the concept.[50] It can also be described as a continuum.

As is the case with all activities that fall in the realm of social science, human inability to conduct social experiments limits the study of war and thus theories of victory. Therefore, the study is relegated to observation and analysis. Determining causality and predictive ability are also severely limited. This points to the importance of context. As Colin Gray describes, "Context

---

[47] J. Boone Bartholomees, 25.

[48] The American Heritage Dictionary, Second College Edition, 1347.

[49] J. Boone Bartholomees, 25 and Brian Bond, 201.

[50] Colin S. Gray, "Defining and Achieving Decisive Victory," v and J. Boone Bartholomees, 26.

rules!"[51] When designing campaigns or major operations, templates are of little use as senior decision makers must treat every enemy as a unique strategic, social, political, and cultural entity.[52] It is also critical to understand what the opponent's theory of victory is and what their perception regarding the eventual outcome actually is.

Victory, then, is very subjective. Bartholomees suggests that victory is an assessment rather than a fact or condition.[53] Victory is not only physical, but also cognitive and moral. The old adage of perception being reality certainly applies to this discussion. There are many interested agents in any conflict who make an assessment of the situation. It is critical to determine whose analysis matters the most, when it matters, why it matters, and what criteria senior leaders will use to determine these issues.[54] For the United States, the assessment of the American people clearly matters most. This idea supports the previously discussed hybrid war threats' use of two of Clausewitz's concepts; will as a source of power and how willpower relates to the United States' center of gravity. Therefore, it is important when constructing a theory of victory to understand who decides what victory means for the enemy and how they decide.

Theory Of Victory = How To Win + What Is Winning

"How To Win"

One of the first tasks senior decision makers must accomplish when developing a theory of victory with regards to hybrid war is to develop a "Way" to defeat adversaries attempting to generate hybrid war while defending oneself. Simply put, it is designing a strategy to combat the challenge of hybrid war. In order for the United States to defeat any threat it must develop a

---

[51] Colin S. Gray, "Recognizing and Understanding Revolutionary Change in War: The Sovereignty of Context," (U.S. Army War College Strategic Studies Institute Monograph, Carlisle Barracks, PA, February 2006), 48.

[52] Ibid., vi.

[53] J. Boone Bartholomees, 25.

[54] Ibid.

theory of victory appropriate for the environment and the threat the United States faces. Developing a sound theory of victory is absolutely critical because, as Colin Gray maintains, "there is more to war than warfare," since "the succeeding peace is the breeding ground for future conflict."[55]

Hybrid war is evolving for many reasons. Paradoxically, U.S. dominance in the conventional realm has been one of the main catalysts for this type of war. In addition to our strengths, potential adversaries have studied the American system of war and understand its weaknesses. Hybrid war is meant to attack American weaknesses at all levels with complex threats, in multiple domains, while avoiding American strengths. The 2006 Israel-Hezbollah war seemed to foreshadow the effects of a hybrid war challenge the United States may face.

Figure 2 depicts three hypothetical hybrid threats mapped on the 2005 National Defense Strategy "Quad Chart."[56] The paradigm the United States has traditionally been comfortable with is the adversary described in the bottom left, the "Traditional" quadrant, although that comfort level now increasingly includes threats in the upper left portion of the chart, the "Irregular" quadrant. Single-mode traditional threats are not the most likely adversaries of the future due to overwhelming U.S. ability to counter traditional threats. It is significant to note that there is no exact form that an adversary operating in a hybrid war takes, as depicted by the three different hybrid war threat forms, "A", "B", and "C". Every scenario will be different, posing unique challenges to the United States. It is also important to note the information operations bubble that

---

[55] Colin S. Gray, *Another Bloody Century: Future Warfare,* 37 and 15.

[56] This chart is an original, created by the author. It uses a graphic depiction of the 4 types of threats found in the 2005 NDS, page 2-6. These threats were often depicted in Pentagon briefs as the, "quad chart." [56] Nathan Freier, "Strategic Competition and Resistance in the 21st Century: Irregular, Catastrophic, Traditional, and Hybrid Challenges in Context." (U.S. Army War College Strategic Studies Institute Monograph, Carlisle Barracks, May 2007), 2-3.

encompasses all three bubbles in a hybrid war context. Fully integrated information operations are noticeably absent from the U.S. construct of possible threats it could face in the future. [57]

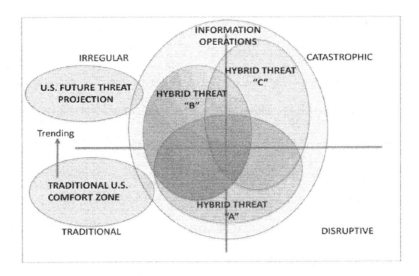

Figure 2. 2005 Hybrid War and Threat Categories

The United States' strategic methodology has concentrated on the difficult process of planning for, coordinating, and executing to achieve Brian Bond's two previously discussed objectives; winning decisive campaign victories and translating those victories into long-term political gains. Added to the difficulty of targeting a hybrid war challenger's means is the American notion of decisive victory and unconditional surrender. It is this idea of absolutes that frames any theory of victory short of total defeat of the enemy as a failure for the United States. [58]

---

[57] It is important to note that the future is actually a metaphor since it does not yet exist and therefore humans can never know it. What strategists are actually doing when "looking to the future," is developing a set of alternatives that allow them to critically examine possible actions, identify imbalances, and ensure they are ready to face issues that may occur. Shimon Naveh, interview by Matt Matthews, Fort Leavenworth, Kansas, November 1, 2007. This is exactly what General Mattis speaks of in his warning to not get the future "too wrong." Mackubin Thomas Owens, 74. Considering the future as metaphor then, hybrid war should be one of the types of threats the United States considers developing a strategy for and ensuring imbalances are minimized.

[58] William C. Martel, *Victory in War: Foundations in Military Policy,* (New York: Cambridge Press, 2007), 106.

This idea of total military victory, which has become the American strategic paradigm, may not be possible in a hybrid war. Understanding the current U.S theory of victory, based primarily on conventional threats, is important to determine how a senior leader will use the military to support political objectives. This awareness will enable the senior decision maker to design a new theory of victory in a hybrid war.

Figure 3 illustrates a paradigm where technology-driven, conventional, joint forces attack the enemy's military to achieve decisive military victory, which in turn influences the enemy's will to continue the fight or quit the fight. Senior decision makers are able to convert victory into a positive, long-term political outcome. This paradigm has its roots in Jominian and Clausewitzian thinking that details defeat of the enemy forces as the key to victory. As Brian Bond maintains however, strategic decisive military victory is very difficult.[59] The concept of decisive military victory is so foundational to the U.S. theory of victory, securing anticipated political outcomes becomes very difficult. Both decisive military victory and a favorable political outcome will become even more difficult in hybrid war.

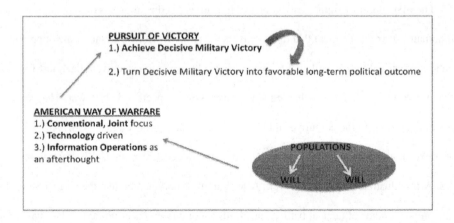

Figure 3. Current U.S. Theory of Victory

---

[59] Brian Bond, 201.

Conversely, adversaries attempting to fight a hybrid war may utilize three main elements to enable it to circumvent the first objective, decisive military victory, and concentrate on the second objective, long-term political victory. As referenced in Figure 4, which depicts the hybrid war theory of victory, three significant elements are the emphasis on the cognitive and moral domains (in addition to using the physical domain), elusive form, and full spectrum warfare capabilities.

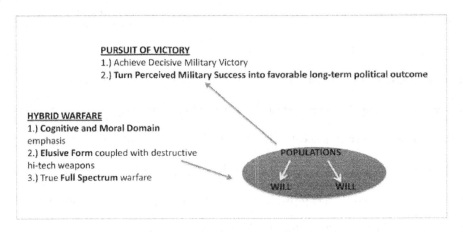

Figure 4. Hybrid War Challenger Theory of Victory

The first and most significant enabler of hybrid war is the emphasis on the cognitive and moral domains. It is this element that drives adversaries in a hybrid war to target the opponent's population, specifically their will, and allows the hybrid warrior to circumvent the quest for decisive military victory. The North Vietnamese understood aspects of hybrid war. They were masters of operations in the cognitive and moral domains during the Vietnam War. An oft-quoted post war exchange between a high-ranking North Vietnamese officer and Col Harry Summers of the U.S. Army illustrates this concept well. After Summers commented that the United States had won the preponderance of tactical battles, the North Vietnamese officer replied, "That may be so, but it is also irrelevant."[60] It is also important to understand that it is very probable in hybrid war that the enemy will insulate its population, and therefore their will, from U.S. influence attempts.

Convincing many different audiences of their defeat makes waging hybrid war especially difficult. As Sun Tzu admonishes to know thy enemy, senior decision makers must design a plan with multiple audiences, possibly from different cultures, in mind. The plan must allow the military to directly or indirectly target the enemy's will so that he realizes and admits defeat, and subsequently ceases operations. As Sun Tzu describes, this military victory will provide effective support for the political establishment.[61]

Second, hybrid war threats constitute an elusive and fluid form. Their strategy directs a great deal of effort in the cognitive and moral domains, but the portion that resides in the physical domain is difficult to find, identify, and target because it often blends into the surrounding environment. This may prolong the conflict, exhausting U.S. will and resources. The blending of military and civilian forms in the physical realm also increases the possibility of U.S. and civilian causalities. This physical problem further exacerbates the battle in the cognitive and moral domains by providing potential fuel for the adversaries' information operations, increasing the possibility of achieving strategic effects.

One example of this fluidity is Saddam Hussein's flexible conventional and irregular use of the Fedayeen during Operation Iraqi Freedom. As allied forces raced for Baghdad in 2003, these fighters began an irregular warfare campaign. Another example is the potential Iranian use of distributed operations at sea. The Iranians deliberately developed the ability to coordinate the use of small, fast surface vessels that blend into the thousands of fishing vessels and commercial traffic in the Persian Gulf. This threat poses a significant risk to U.S. naval forces because it is extremely difficult to identify friend from foe. This increases the probability that an adversary can

---

[60] J. Boone Bartholomees, 26.

[61] Sun Tzu, *The Art of War.* trans. J.H. Huang, 109.

use an engagement in the physical realm to explicitly influence the cognitive and moral domains. The March 2008 accidental killing of an Egyptian fisherman by U.S. merchantmen in the Suez Canal is evidence of this difficulty.[62]

The elusive and flexible form of adversaries waging hybrid war makes identification and targeting difficult, especially considering that the U.S. theory of victory rests upon decisive military victory. Additionally, elusive form, coupled with new ways to use terrain (especially urban terrain), make collateral damage a significant factor. The hybrid warrior's strategy capitalizes on collateral damage mistakes the United States makes in the cognitive and moral domains. Using this form in dense urban terrain may also produce U.S. casualties that an adversary can use in the cognitive and moral domains of hybrid war against the U.S. public. Operating in a high-threat, often distributed, urban environment also effects U.S. soldiers in the moral domain by increasing fear and decreasing cohesion, morale, and will.

The last element that characterizes hybrid war is true full spectrum warfare capabilities. Globalization, the spread of affordable information technology, cyberwar means, and readily available, advanced off-the-shelf armaments eliminates the United States' near-monopoly on technologically sophisticated capabilities. It is not merely the access to the means, but the ability to apply these means in a number of different modes, realms, domains, and levels of war simultaneously that makes this threat extremely relevant to the United States. Hezbollah's use of cell phones to coordinate targeting of Israeli tanks using conventional anti-tank rounds and improvised explosive devices by guerrilla fighters in 2006 is an excellent example of this blending at the tactical level.

The use of hybrid war's true full spectrum means will be extremely challenging to the United States. This presents the United States with a problem set analogous to the one it intends

---

[62] "U.S. admits to Suez Canal Killing," *ABC News*, March 26, 2008. http://www.abc.net.au/news/stories/2008/03/26/2200141.htm (accessed September 23, 2008).

to present its adversaries, parallel operations across many different realms. This full spectrum threat may attempt to manipulate the propensities of different complex systems such as the economy, environment, and information infrastructure, to their advantage. The United States may not have the ability to bring these systems back within an acceptable level of tolerance. All three of these points share one theme, the importance of both sides' will and how each point either directly or indirectly influences the will of significant agents in the system. Influencing the adversary's will remains a vital part of the hybrid warrior's strategy.

There is an important balance that must be struck between the enemy's means and his will, Clausewitz's two elements of victory.[63] Both must be defeated to some degree, but "Destroying the enemy's means without breaking his will leaves you with a less capable but still hostile foe."[64] The key to victory then, is to break the adversary's will.[65] Modern examples that support this theory include the seeds of World War II that were sown in the aftermath of World War I. A bad peace significantly contributed to a second world war. This is also true of Operation Iraqi Freedom and Operation Desert Storm. Both these conflicts destroyed a great deal of the enemy's military capacity, but did not diminish the "defeated" powers' will. Failure to defeat Germany and Iraq in the cognitive and moral domains set the conditions for future conflicts.

Because of the United States' Clausewitzian view that its military must defeat the adversary's forces to impose its will, the United States will likely have difficulty with hybrid war just as Israel did against Hezbollah in 2006, unless it adjusts its strategy. Ralph Peters noted,

---

[63] Carl von Clausewitz, 77.

[64] J. Boone Bartholomees, 35.

[65] Ibid.

"Israel fought as a limping stepchild of Clausewitz. Hezbollah fought as Sun Tzu's fanatical son."[66]

The United States has found it very difficult to diminish the will of its adversaries directly, though.[67] This has led to U.S. targeting of the enemy's military means as a way to indirectly influence the adversary's will. It may be more difficult to target adversaries' means in a hybrid war because of the elusive and flexible forms they are likely to take. Also, a great deal of the means employed in hybrid war affect the cognitive and moral domains, including attempts to directly target their adversaries' will. Examples of this skill set include North Vietnamese use of American media to directly target U.S. public will during the Vietnam War and the National Liberation Front's use of newspapers and news magazines to directly target French public will during the Algerian insurgency.

Most recently, irregular adversaries of the United States in the Middle East have used Al Jazeerah, other news outlets, and the internet, to target both U.S. and Muslim will. These examples of irregular threat "doctrine" illustrate the idea that hybrid war is indeed a hybrid of different theories of war, as previously discussed. This direct-targeting mindset is antithetical to the American way of war, grounded in Clausewitzian and Jominian ideas that call for defeat of the enemy's military forces as the key to victory.

Author Michael Vlahos states that, "success is all about how our rule-sets mesh with the enemy" with rule sets being how we, "do military operations, but also how we understand our enterprise as a success."[68] In fact, Vlahos maintains that, "enemy buy-in to our war frame *has*

---

[66] Ralph Peters, "Lessons from Lebanon: The New Model Terrorist Army," *Armed Forces Journal* (October, 2006), http://www.armedforcesjournal.com/2006/10/2069044/ (accessed January 18, 2009).

[67] Targeting the enemy's will directly typically requires direct targeting of the leadership and or citizens of the adversary nation. The former is difficult due to U.S. policy as well as intelligence and force requirements, the latter because the will of the people has shown to be very resilient to targeting. Examples include targeting Saddam Hussein, a valid military command and control target, and the German people during the Combined Bomber Offensive during World War II.

always been the critical and unacknowledged factor in American battle success."[69] By comparing

Figure 3, the current U.S. theory of victory, to Figure 4, the hybrid war theory of victory, it is

clear that in hybrid war, the enemy's rule-sets do not match the United States rule-sets. As an

example, rule sets do not mesh in the Middle East today. This will present problems for the

United States if faced with a hybrid threat in the future. This is especially true if their rule-sets

make the United States' resistance to them beneficial for them and counterproductive for the

United States.[70] The goal, then, is to develop a strategy that works to the U.S.' advantage, not

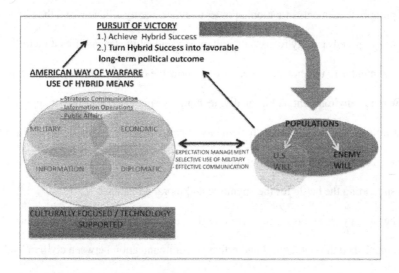

Figure 5. "How to Win" in Hybrid War

the adversaries' advantage. Figure 5 describes a general framework of a strategy designed to

defeat a threat attempting to wage hybrid war. As retired U.S. Marine Corps Lieutenant Colonel

Frank Hoffman explains, the United States understands how to design operational level strategies

for conventional enemies and is regaining understanding about how to design operational level

---

[68] Michael Vlahos, "Fighting Identity: Why We Are Losing Our Wars," *Military Review,* (November-December 2007): 4.

[69] Ibid.

[70] Michael Vlahos, 4.

strategies for irregular threats.[71] The United States has not attempted to adapt a strategy to the hybrid challenge, at the strategic or operational level. Sun Tzu's recommendations to attack the enemy system will be used as a construct to develop a U.S. theory of victory in hybrid war.

Generally speaking, the theory of victory will attack the first three portions of the enemy system. The preponderance of effort is allocated against the enemy strategy by being culturally focused, having a strategy that supports the battle in the cognitive and moral domains, and protects the U.S.' critical vulnerability, the public will. The U.S.' hybrid war theory of victory uses the appropriate elements of national power to attack enemy alliances and then its military.

This proposed strategy focuses on culture since identity is a significant factor in war today.[72] The intent is to understand the enemy and how the enemy understands himself, and thus interacts with the environment. Additionally, technology should support the strategy, not the other way around. The strategy uses all elements of national power, with the battle for the cognitive domain being the enveloping, fully integrated theme. In essence, it is a decisive hybrid approach supporting the battle for the cognitive and moral domains.

The strategy also calls for protection of the public will, the U.S.' critical vulnerability. This is accomplished through honest and effective communication between civilian leadership, senior military leadership, the American people and allies, as well as judicious use of the military instrument. This strategy will allow the United States to influence the adversaries' will so they capitulate. Defining "what is winning" and turning it into lasting political gains is the next step.

---

[71] Frank G. Hoffman, "Hybrid Warfare and Challengers." *Joint Forces Quarterly.* (1st Quarter 2009): 38.

[72] Michael Vlahos, 11.

Theory Of Victory = How To Win + What Is Winning

"What Is Winning"

Determining "what is winning" is the most difficult portion of developing any theory of victory and without it the senior decision maker's design is "woefully incomplete."[73] Determining "what is winning" may be even more difficult in hybrid war. The 2008/2009 Israeli war with Hamas illustrates this difficulty. Steven Erlanger of the New York Times notes of the Israeli problem, "it remains far from clear how to decide when to end the war, and what would constitute victory."[74]

Generically, "winning" can be considered as the conditions set for the system of interest to be self-regulating in the U.S.' best interest, for some explicit amount of time, without undermining U.S. credibility, legitimacy, will, relationships, and resources. "Winning" is a continuum, not a static end state, and must concentrate on long-term conditions vice short-term gains. In other words, it is the vision of the complex system that the senior decision maker desires. Former Undersecretary of Defense for Policy, Fred Charles Ikle', maintains that the most decisive long-term influence on a conflict is how it concludes.[75] How the conflict concludes is dependant on conditions that are set well before hostilities begin. It is imperative then, to develop the best understanding possible of "what is winning" before the conflict begins and to adapt as necessary during hostilities.

As mentioned, the theory of victory is contextual and therefore is suitable for a number of guiding principles vice rigid laws. Since national security literature does not widely address this topic (the last act in the drama of war as described by Ikle') a general theory of victory will be

---

[73] Fred Charles Ikle', *Every War Must End* (New York: Columbia University Press, 1991), 1.

[74] Steven Erlanger, "For Israel, 2006 Lessons but Old Pitfalls," *The New York Times,* 7 Jan 2009, http://www.nytimes.com/2009/01/07/world/middleeast/07military.html (accessed January 18, 2009).

[75] Fred Charles Ikle', vii.

discussed and then hybrid war implications will be addressed using the general theory of victory as comparison criteria.[76]

Victory is dependant on how one defines the problem, which senior leaders frame while developing the resolution. The theory of victory for a certain conflict must be flexible and dynamic, changing with the context and emergent problems, opportunities, and conditions of the conflict. It is absolutely critical to make the theory of victory and its inherently dynamic nature explicit so that senior leaders can manage expectations. Expectation management is crucial in a democracy where the critical vulnerability is the people's will.

The theory of victory developed by senior leaders may be very broad, covering a large number of different concepts that span the diplomatic, information, military, economic (DIME) instruments of national power, in all three domains. As Bar-Yam maintains, complexity must be met with complexity.[77] It includes consideration of what the enemy theory of victory is postulated to be, mission success criteria, clear military and national strategic objectives and desired states, war termination criteria, conflict resolution, security, stability, and reconstruction efforts (if necessary), U.S. domestic conditions, negotiating leverage, relationships, regional and international institutions, post-war settlements, risk, and costs.[78]

---

[76] Fred Charles Ikle', 4.

[77] Yaneer Bar-Yam, *Making Things Work: Solving Complex Problems in a Complex World,* (Cambridge: Knowledge Press, 2004), 91.

[78] Significantly, many think that conflict termination equals victory. As mentioned, conflict termination is only part of a theory of victory. One example that illustrates this is the situation at the "conclusion" of World War I. From a conventional sense, the conflict was terminated since the belligerents stopped fighting one another (on a grand scale), but the Allies, while crowned victors, did not achieve victory. Using Clausewitz's framework for resistance as being the combination of means and will is helpful. While a portion of Germany's means were exhausted, there was still a great deal of fighting means left. Clearly, their will was not exhausted either. Many of the Allies realized that victory was not achieved. An excerpt from John Mosier's book, "The Myth of the Great War" clearly shows this, "Petain realized-as did Pershing-that Germany was nowhere beaten, nor would it be until the German Army had been...The Germans, who wanted to preserve their army and their military cadre intact, saw an opportunity for doing that by dealing with Wilson." John Mosier, *The Myth of the Great War: A New Military History of World War I* (New York: Harper Collins Publishers, 2001), 335. Additionally, General Marshall commented that

Senior decision makers must understand, to the best of their ability, what the enemy's theory of victory is, and incorporate this understanding into their own theory of victory. For Hezbollah in 2006, survival meant victory. Understanding the logic that supports this theory, and the subsequent enemy narrative, is critical in shaping one's own theory of victory. This will help shape the friendly logic and narrative.[79] It is also important to understand that the notion of victory is cultural. This is especially true in the temporal dimension of the theory of victory as Middle and Far Eastern cultures have a much different understanding of time than do Western cultures.

Joint doctrine covers many of the other concepts encompassed in the theory of victory. The risks and costs include determining the hazards of peace, not just the hazards of war.[80] The United States must maintain or restore its legitimacy and credibility. This is significant because relationships with many different agents in the world system will change during and after the conflict based on new realities. The United States must sustain its ability to deter, as well as sustain its will and resources. Additionally, senior decision makers must strive to design a resolution that provides the adversary system a positive attractor so that its propensity gravitates towards the U.S. desired state. This will help ensure a greater threat does not emerge after the initial problem is resolved.

---

he thought, "the Germans should have been sufficiently "licked" to scotch the myth that their government accepted peace without defeat in the field." Forest C. Pogue, *George C. Marshall: Education of a General 1880-1939,* (New York: Viking Press, 1963), 193. It is also important to realize that these experiences helped shape thinking about victory during World War II. The quest for German and Japanese unconditional surrender in part stemmed from the World War I experience. General Omar Bradley, one of the most successful U.S. Army commanders during World War II commented, "We shall never stop until the [German] army is beaten and until the army knows it is beaten. I shall never discuss terms. I shall insist on an unconditional surrender immediately." Carlo D'Este, *Decision in Normandy* (New York: E.P. Dutton, Inc., 1983), 405.

[79] The theory of victory will help inform the United States' strategic narrative that will be designed to dominate the enemy's narrative. It is also important to understand that there will be two different narratives from two different strategic cultures. Paradoxically, the narrative designed to fight against and achieve political objectives against a hybrid warrior will use some of their logic against them.

[80] Fred Charles Ikle', 7.

Lieutenant General von der Goltz of the Prussian Army described a portion of "winning" when he stated, "It is, above all things, necessary to satisfy ourselves as to whether our own military power is sufficient, after victory on the battle-field, to cause the enemy's country to feel the burden of war severely enough to desire a return to peace."[81] However, von der Goltz's concept is incomplete since warfare must serve war, not itself. Determining what the peace should "look like" and why is a critical responsibility of the senior decision maker. Once again, war is a strategic concept while warfare is a tactical concept. As an example, Napoleon was undoubtedly one of the great military geniuses of all time. He was however, unable to turn operational success into strategic long-term gains. Napoleon was an expert at warfare, not at the conduct of war. As Ikle' maintains, it is the outcome of war, not campaigns, that decides how well the endeavor meets the national interests.[82]

Unfortunately, in the past, the United States has fallen into the same trap that Napoleon fell into many times by not defining victory and working towards a strategic goal. Instead, the American way of war, as described by Weigley, seeks to destroy the enemy's military instead of serving as an extension of policy, as Clausewitz maintains.[83] This mindset incorrectly equates winning battles to winning wars and is based on a faulty concept of victory.[84] Vietnam should

---

[81] Freiherr Von der Goltz, *The Conduct of War: A Short Treatise on its Most Important Branches and Guiding Rules* (London: Kegan Paul, Trench, Trubner and Co, Ltd, 1908), 19. A recommended modification to account for current context would be to substitute instruments of national power for military, but it is an excellent summation of a significant portion of "what is winning."

[82] Fred Charles Ikle', 2.

[83] Russell F. Weigley, *The American Way of War: A History of United States Military Strategy and Policy* (Bloomington: Indiana University Press, 1973), xxii and Carl von Clausewitz, *On War*, 87.

[84] Antulio J. Echevarria II, "Toward an American Way of War," (U.S. Army War College Strategic Studies Institute Monograph, Carlisle Barracks, PA, March 2004), 2.

have proven this point and Iraq should have provided a reminder. Unfortunately, the American way of war tends to ignore the difficult process of turning military success into strategic gains.[85]

This task is extremely difficult because it requires some level of predictive capability, which is marginal at best in a complex wartime environment. The interconnectedness of the many agents of this system, many of whom exhibit non-linear, complex behavior, make this an almost impossible task both before and during engagement. It is important to at least weigh the significant uncertainties to determine if it is advantageous to start a conflict or adopt another approach to achieve political objectives.[86]

At the strategic level, victory means achieving political objectives and it is significant to understand that perceptions matter. Each side will have their idea of what reality is and the total of both sets of reality is not a zero-sum-game.[87] Lebanese Brigadier General Hanna noted of Hezbollah during Hezbollah's 2006 war with Israel that it may be impossible to truly judge victory with an actor such as Hezbollah, also suggesting that Israel achieved no political goals.[88] Another Lebanese officer, Lt Col Hany Nakhleh, stated that both sides thought they were winning and therefore it was not easy to determine who the final winner and loser were.[89] J. Boone Bartholomees provides a useful scale (Figure 6) with which to conceptualize success. Using this scale, Israel ends up in the "Not win" to "Lose" portion of Bartholomees' scale of success and Hezbollah in the "Win" portion of the scale.

---

[85] Ibid., 7.

[86] Fred Charles Ikle', 20.

[87] Michael I. Handel, *Masters of War: Classical Strategic Thought, 3rd ed.* (New York: Frank Cass Publishers, 2004), 197.

[88] Elias Hanna, 89 and 86.

[89] Hany T. Nakhleh, "The 2006 Israeli War on Lebanon: Analysis and Strategic Implications," (U.S. Army War College Strategy Research Project, 2007), 7.

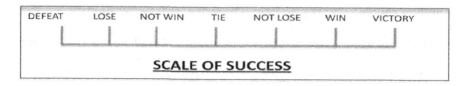

Figure 6. Bartholomees' Scale of Success

Other recent examples of contested victories include the 1973 Arab-Israeli War and the First Gulf War. Both sides in both conflicts had very different concepts of who won. The struggles and conflicts that followed suggest that formulating a theory of victory before and during the conflict is paramount. As both Clausewitz and Galula describe, results of war are never final.[90] Also significant is the fact that one's opponent must both realize and admit their defeat. The popular French resistance to von Moltke's advance to Paris in 1870 after the Prussians soundly defeated the French army illustrates this concept of accepting defeat (or not).[91]

The concept of reconciliation is another important principle in determining what winning is. The enemy must be defeated and they must understand they are defeated, but the enemy must be treated well enough during deliberation at the end of a conflict. This mindset will avoid unnecessary devastation that may lead to a loss of domestic and allied support, as well as create new enemies.[92] In a globalized world, this concept is critical. Bismarck is an excellent example of a senior decision maker who understood that today's enemy has the potential to be tomorrow's ally, and vice versa. History has shown that enemies are seldom permanent.[93]

---

[90] Carl von Clausewitz, 80 and David Galula, *Counterinsurgency War: Theory and Practice* (St Petersburg: Hailer Publishing, 1964), 137.

[91] Brian Bond, 71-73.

[92] Fred Charles Ikle', xi.

[93] Ibid., 11.

During this process of determining "what is winning," it is critical to understand what the enemy's value of the "object" is, as Clausewitz described.[94] The enemy's logic will drive the value of whatever "object" they fight for. Senior decision makers must also consider the U.S. value of the "object". Current context influences both belligerents. One pertinent, current example is the issue of Taiwan in relations between the United States and China, a potential challenger that could attempt to wage hybrid war. Considering the current U.S. commitments to Iraq and Afghanistan, as well as the current economic situation, Taiwan may mean more to China, who considers Taiwan a legitimate part of its country, than to the United States. Understanding, to the best of one's ability, the adversary's value of the "object" will help determine what the enemy's idea of winning will be. This determination will comprise part of their logic, which will, in turn, drives their strategic narrative. Understanding the enemy narrative follows Sun Tzu's admonition that to be victorious requires one to know thy enemy.

When designing a theory of victory, senior decision makers must be flexible in their thinking, as the theory of victory must be flexible. The U.S. Marine Corps Information Paper that addresses hybrid war states that an organization must be "agile and adaptive in its approach."[95] The understanding of "what is winning" is never a finished product because it is the result of a flexible mindset that has the ability to be adjusted based on the current and anticipated context. It is also important to realize, as Michael Handel points out, that, "even the best theory does not hold all of the answers."[96] It will only be a theory, not a rule, since it lives in the world of social science. It is akin to a hypothesis that will be tested and modified again and again. As such,

---

[94] Carl von Clausewitz, 92.

[95] U.S. Marine Corps, *SVG Strategic Trends and Implications* (Strategic Vision Group Information Paper, 12 February 2008), 4.

[96] Michael I. Handel, 43.

measures of success will help senior decision makers understand when to adjust the theory of victory.

The theory of victory will also serve to generate dialogue between the political leadership and senior military leadership to help fill the discourse space, as described by Kobi Michael.[97] Filling this space will help generate the intellectual rigor that is vital to resolve the complex problems that hybrid war presents. It will also help identify where, along the "victory continuum," senior decision makers anticipate a conflict to culminate.

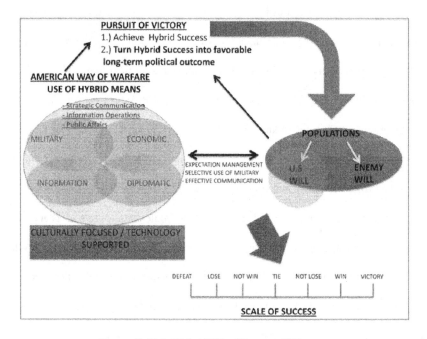

Figure 7. U.S. Hybrid War Theory of Victory

---

[97] Kobi Michael, "The Dilemma Behind the Classical Dilemma of Civil-Military Relations: The "Discourse Space" Model and the Israeli Case During the Oslo Process," *Armed Forces and Society* 33, no 4 (July 2007), 518. The discourse space is a construct developed by Kobi Michael to describe the thinking and communication that is necessary to occur between political leaders and senior military officers. Filling this "space" with appropriate dialogue and discussion will help lead to a shared understanding of the situation and an effective way to resolve problems.

Who is responsible for designing a relevant concept of "what is winning" for the situation of interest? It is the senior decision maker that develops and communicates this vision to all applicable organizations in the friendly system. This common vision will provide the bounds for all supporting strategies.

Differences In Hybrid War - "What Is Winning"

The principles of "what is winning" are useful criteria to compare and contrast the concept of "what is winning" with respect to hybrid war. As previously mentioned, it is important to understand that theories of victory are contextual. Each type of war will have a different theory of victory, as will each conflict, regardless of what type of war it is. A theory of victory for an irregular war will differ from a nuclear theory of victory. Also, the theory of victory for Iraq will be different than the theory of victory for Afghanistan, the Philippines, or any other conflict that may emerge.

Something as seemingly simple as defining the problem becomes part of the problem in hybrid war. Because of its very nature, hybrid war presents a complex problem. Aspects of this complexity include emphasis on the cognitive and moral domain, elusive form, true full spectrum warfare, and a variety of different actors that combine to pose a different threat in each specific scenario. These different aspects make it difficult to impose political control during the ensuing peace. The different entities that comprise the overall hybrid threat in a certain conflict may have different political concerns or none at all. Additionally, the different entities may fight for different objects or place different values on the same objects they fight for. The United States may affect one entity differently in the cognitive and moral domains than another.[98]

All these possibilities will lead to emerging hybrid strategies, making the senior decision maker's job of understanding the adversary very difficult. Determining whose will matters most

---

[98] These complexities may however, lead to tensions in the adversary system that can be exploited by the United States.

and how to affect that will is problematic. It is clear that defining the problem in a hybrid war must be the first task senior decision makers resolve.

While the senior leader attempts to define the problem hybrid war presents, he simultaneously designs a resolution to the problem.[99] Attaining victory in a hybrid war does not necessarily mean solving a complex problem, but rather resolving a complex problem to an acceptable level, as Rittel and Webber maintain.[100] The senior decision maker must understand that they may have to address the problem posed by a hybrid war at a later time, but often in a different manner because the context has changed. The goal is to inject energy into the system to work with the system's propensities and potential to drive it into a self-regulating state.

The U.S. Army Commander's Appreciation and Campaign Design (CACD) concept describes a self-regulating system as one that requires no outside interference or control.[101] It is more helpful to understand a self-regulating state as a continuum that exists in the U.S.' zone of tolerance, instead of the absolute concept that CACD recommends. The senior decision maker must make this zone of tolerance explicit before hostilities begin and remain flexible during the conflict.

---

[99] Rittel and Webber maintain that in order to describe and understand a "wicked" or complex problem, one must simultaneously develop possible resolutions to the problem. "Problem understanding and problem resolution are concomitant to each other." Horst W. J. Rittel and Melvin M. Webber, "Dilemmas in a General Theory of Planning," (modified paper presented to the Panel on Policy Sciences, American Association for the Advancement of Science, Boston, MA, December, 1969), 161.

[100] Rittel and Webber also maintain that problems cannot be solved, but resolved. "Social problems are never solved. At best they are only re-solved—over and over again." Since war is social relationship between belligerents, there can never be a perfect solution to war. Human nature and the complexity inherent in human behavior means that the problem one attempts to solve will most likely surface again, albeit in another form. Horst W. J. Rittel and Melvin M. Webber, 160.

[101] U.S. Army, *Commander's Appreciation and Campaign Design,* TRADOC Pamphlet 525-5-500, Fort Monroe, VA: Headquarters Department of the Army Training and Doctrine Command, 28 January 2008, 42.

Often, as the current U.S. situation in Iraq illustrates, the definition of problem resolution becomes "good enough" as time, patience, and resources are expended.[102] Many factors contribute to the concept of problem resolution. These factors may be internal to the adversary system, internal to the friendly system, or external to both. For example, another problem with a higher priority may emerge, similar to the anticipated shift of emphasis from the Iraqi Area of Operations to the Afghan Area of Operations. The perception that the situation in Afghanistan (a perceived higher threat to U.S. national interests) is deteriorating, while the situation in Iraq appears to be stabilizing, helps cause the Iraq situation to emerge as being resolved.

Additionally, since complex problems can only be resolved, not solved, victory has a temporal aspect because the understanding of it changes over time. While military success may be readily apparent, as Ikle' states, the verdict will emerge later in the political arena.[103] This is mainly because senior decision makers can never truly understand the whole system and are unable to predict causality in much of the system. What many consider victory at one time may not constitute victory later as more understanding or second and third order effects emerge. Thus, complex causal relationships contribute to an infinite time horizon.

Therefore, victory is a long-term concept, not a short-term one. It may not be permanent, or perfect. The emergence of the Cold War after "successful" termination of World War II is one example of this concept since the Allied theory of victory did not include half of Europe dominated by communism, in addition to communism's incipient spread around the world

Once again, Bartholemees' scale of success is useful in evaluating where along the conflict continuum a hybrid war may lie, both before and during the conflict. This evaluation must match the senior decision maker's zone of tolerance or else that senior leader must adjust the zone of tolerance. Due to many aspects of hybrid war discussed in the "how to win" chapter, the

---

[102] Horst W. J. Rittel and Melvin M. Webber, 162.

[103] Fred Charles Ikle', viii.

evaluation of the conflict may be further to the left of the continuum than the United States is used to. The disparity between these rule-sets in hybrid war and those of the United States make the outcome of a conflict less certain than previous conflicts and therefore puts the United States in unfamiliar territory.

If a hybrid war is necessary, it is critical for the senior decision maker to set and manage expectations. These expectations include those of the legislature, military, inter-agency, and the American public. Communicating these expectations, as well as the concept that the expectations may change as the conflict progresses, is an important part of the senior decision maker's task. The senior decision maker's ability to articulate these concepts may be the difference between attaining victory and not attaining victory as American will ebbs and flows over the course of the conflict. The senior decision maker must set the domestic strategic conditions to maintain the will and support of the people, or support a shift in the mindset of the American people if that will has begun to erode.

As discussed earlier, understanding the enemy's theory of victory and culture is paramount. This is extremely difficult in a hybrid war because the enemy system is complex and adaptive. It may include state, non-state, and even criminal actors. This will make understanding hybrid war even more difficult and thus defining a theory of victory difficult as well. As in the case of Hezbollah in 2006, survival of the movement meant victory. How will the United States develop a theory of victory against an enemy whose will may be extremely difficult to target, its elusive form may prevent decisive military victory, and its concept of "what is winning" is simply survival? An adversary of this nature may be successful against the United States because of who the United States is and what survival in the context of their theory of victory means.[104] These ideas will force the United States to also become adaptive if it wishes to prevail.

---

[104] Michael Vlahos, 5.

Additionally, because of the emphasis on the cognitive and moral domains in hybrid war, defining victory in the minds of many different audiences will be a complex, challenging task. As noted earlier, perceptions matter. Even determining whose perceptions matter is a difficult prospect. Once again, the strategic outcome of the 2006 Israeli-Hezbollah war is open to debate. As time progresses, there has even been debate on whether Russia was actually victorious against Georgia in 2008.[105]

Conclusion

Michael Evans describes the current complex world as a bifurcated strategic environment that demands full spectrum strategy.[106] Additionally, as Michele Flournoy, Under Secretary of Defense for Policy, and Shawn Brimley state, "Hybrid warfare will be a defining feature of the future security environment."[107] Nowhere is this more significant than in the task of developing a theory of victory. A theory of victory is the foundation of any approach to solving a political problem with military means, and is different for each type of war and each individual conflict. It

---

[105] Although Russia may have achieved tactical success against Georgia in August 2008, many are beginning to consider the invasion a strategic loss for Russia. "Yet, while Russia won the war in tactical and operational terms, it is fast becoming clear to Moscow-as it should have been before the war-that Russia's strategic losses are mounting and will in time eclipse the gains Russia obtained through the use of force." Also noted by Blank, " those who...actually use force, may initially crown themselves victors in such conflicts. Moscow may convince itself that it has won a war in Georgia, but it has actually opened a Pandora's Box of cascading negative effects." Stephen J. Blank, "Georgia: The War Russia Lost," *Military Review* (November-December 2008): 39 and 46. Additionally, U.S. Secretary of State, Condoleezza Rice maintains that Russia has already paid for its overreach into Georgia. She stated that, "Russia's reputation as a potential partner in international institutions - diplomatic, political, security, economic, is frankly in tatters." U.S. Secretary of State, Condoleezza Rice, interview on NBC Meet the Press, August 18, 2008. http://www.america.gov/st/texttransenglish/2008/August/20080818162102bpuh0.257107.html. (accessed January 22, 2009). An important question is whether the Russians agree with these assessments.

[106] Michael Evans, "From the Long Peace to the Long War: Armed Conflict and Military Education and Training in the 21st Century," 9.

[107] Michele A. Flournoy and Shawn Brimley, "The Defense Inheritance: Challenge and Choices for the Next Pentagon Team," *Washington Quarterly* (Autumn 2008): 63.

is the intellectual framework that allows the United States to "seal the strategic deal" and should encompass many different concepts, many of which are already outlined in different contexts.

It appears the United States may be preparing itself to fight the last war. Ironically, this very mindset is typically what the military is heavily critiqued for, and rightly so. It is exactly this type of single mode of warfare mindset that led to many of the problems during the early stages of the insurgencies in Iraq and Afghanistan, only then it was a conventional warfare mindset that hindered successful operations. Counterinsurgency warfare may be shaping the current generation of American officers' experiences and mindsets, possibly leading to an imbalanced perspective of the future. Even the President's defense agenda explicitly outlines stability and counterinsurgency national security challenges as "21st century tasks."[108] It does not mention hybrid or even nuclear threats.

There are others who believe conventional adversaries will threaten the United States in the future. Both these "camps" are incorrect and exemplify an exclusive attitude instead of a necessarily balanced inclusive attitude. The United States must prepare itself to meet myriad challenges, irregular, nuclear, conventional, and hybrid. Implementing an approach to counter these different threats is admittedly difficult. It will require a great deal of intellectual rigor, vision, compromise, and cooperation among many agents in the United States national security system to be successful in today's challenging security environment.

The emerging theme in today's complex security environment is the significance of the cognitive and moral domains. Modern history has witnessed the ultimate aim of military activity, achieving political gains, change many times. The military objective has changed from simply outmaneuvering the opponent, to taking territory, to the Jominian and Clausewitzian ideals of

---

[108] Additionally, when discussing defense programs, the President outlines being ready to fight only conventional, stability, and counterinsurgency threats. Barak Obama, "2009 National Defense Agenda," http://www.whitehouse.gov/agenda/defense (accessed January 29, 2009).

destroying the enemy's armed forces.[109] It may well be transitioning in the 21st century to the ability to defeat an adversary in the cognitive and moral domains without defeating them in the physical domain.

Arguably, the ability to defeat an adversary in the cognitive and moral domains has always been key to counterinsurgency, but it also has strong potential to be the key for other forms of war such as hybrid war. There has been a noticeable shift in enemies of the United States from the primacy of military operations supported very little by information operations, to information operations supported by military operations.[110] There are some in the United States military, such as U.S. Army Colonel William Darley, who favor this approach as well.[111] Emphasizing the cognitive and moral domains in certain contexts may be one key to a sound strategic theory of victory in a hybrid war.[112] It is worth the time and effort to investigate this concept for possible use in U.S. military endeavors. This mindset shift would also help the United States move away from a way of battle to a true way of war by concentrating intellectual rigor on developing a theory of victory both before and during a conflict.

---

[109] Freiherr Von der Goltz, 5 and Azar Gat, *The Origins of Military Thought from the Enlightenment to Clausewitz* (Oxford: Clarendon Press, 1989), 115.

[110] T.X. Hammes, "Fourth Generation Warfare Evolves, Fifth Emerges," 14.

[111] William M. Darley, "Clausewitz's Theory of War and Information Operations." *Joint Forces Quarterly 40,* (1st Quarter 2006): 78.

[112] Although elements of all three domains are constantly interacting and influencing one another, there are times when one domain may be predominant. While it may be impossible to objectively measure this, many practitioners and theoreticians have made subjective judgments. Napoleon commented that the moral is the physical as three is to one, quoted in J.F.C.Fuller, 134. While this may not be a definitive rule, it may be the case in certain contexts. James Schneider commented that, "the moral element of combat remains decisive because in essence combat remains a clash of wills." James Schneider, 2. Clausewitz discusses moral factors and elements, which he states, "are among the most important in war" and, "the physical seem little more than the wooden hilt, while the moral factors are the precious metal, the real weapon, the finely-honed blade." Carl von Clausewitz, 184-185. J.F.C. Fuller states, "Mental force does not win a war; moral force does not win a war, physical force does not win a war; but what *does* win a war is the highest combination of these three forces acting as *one* force." J.F.C. Fuller, 146. A significant task for the senior decision maker (as well as the operational artist) is to determine what that combination is.

Considering the identity and meaning of different agents in the system is also critical. This will ensure these issues are made explicit. Defeating adversaries waging hybrid war will demand the consideration of both the U.S. and enemy identity and meaning from multiple different perspectives.

Another significant aspect of developing a theory of victory with respect to the complexities hybrid war presents is that the United States must meet these complexities with its own complexities. This threat calls for a joint, multi-agency approach that exhibits distributed organization and capabilities across multiple domains. It also necessitates an understanding of hybrid war at all three levels of war that leads to relevant intellectual rigor, as well as action. Fighting a hybrid war threat using the threat's hybrid war concepts against them seems to have potential. As Brig Gen (R) Shimon Naveh states, "complex problems tend to be resolved by combined methods."[113]

The United States has been historically slow to respect its enemies and their type of war.[114] This is a danger in a hybrid war, because the consequences could be grave. There have been many significant modern failures of strategy formulation, including the British invasion of the Dardanelles in 1915, as depicted in *The Perils of Amateur Strategy*, and the U.S. conflict in Vietnam.[115] Developing a sound theory of victory may prevent failures of this magnitude in the

---

[113] Shimon Naveh, *In Pursuit of Military Excellence: The Evolution of Operational Theory,* (New York: Frank Cass, 1997), 50.

[114] Colin S. Gray, "Defining and Achieving Decisive Victory," 29.

[115] In 1915, in order to break the stalemate on the Western front and relieve pressure on Russia on the Eastern front, the Allies (mainly a British effort) attempted an ill-fated invasion of Gallipoli Peninsula. It was designed to control the strait so the British navy could open a Sea Line of Communication to Russia, as well as attack Istanbul and induce the garrison there to revolt, thus ending Turkish involvement and providing a new axis with which to attack Germany. This effort was quickly mired down and resulted in significant loss of Allied manpower, resources, and credibility. It was mainly the result of faulty strategic and operational thinking. Sir Gerald Ellison, *The Perils of Amateur Strategy: As Exemplified by the Attack on the Dardanelles Fortress in 1915* (New York: Longmans, Green, and Co. Ltd., 1926).

future by helping to frame and resolve the problem effectively and efficiently, or to prevent military involvement in the conflict from the beginning.

In a recent speech to the National War College, Secretary of Defense Robert Gates briefly addressed hybrid war as a possibility, but focused on the tactical aspects.[116] Later in the speech he discussed, in general, the concepts of humility and the understanding of one's limits. Connecting these two concepts with hybrid war may be the key to framing a sound theory of victory. Interestingly, the United States military has added restraint to its Principles of War. While engaged in a hybrid war, this is exactly what may help define the U.S. theory of victory since the costs may be too high for the benefits associated with victory.

Developing a sound theory of victory may also lead to a more realistic and disciplined use of the U.S. military and a demilitarization of U.S. foreign policy. There may be situations where the United States can apply military force, but should not. A sound theory of victory will help identify these situations. There may also be situations, like the opening vignette describes, when the United States is compelled to act. Developing a theory of victory for these situations will increase the chances that strategic objectives are met.

Recommendations

This paper recommends that the hybrid war theory of victory outlined earlier serve as starting point for an expanded and improved theory of victory for consideration in the event of a hybrid war. In order to accomplish this, the United States must undertake many efforts. As Brigadier General Krause states, "War takes preparation, whether it is the production of equipment, the training and readiness of forces, or the strategy and policies that guide action."[117]

---

[116] Robert Gates, U.S. Secretary of Defense, Speech to the National Defense University, Washington, D.C., September 29, 2008.

[117] Michael G. Krause, "Square Pegs for Round Holes: Current Approaches to Future War and the Need to Adapt." *Land War Studies Center Working Paper No. 132,* Duntroon Australia, June 2007, 2.

Part of that preparation is developing a theory of victory for the many threats the United States faces. Areas of future study include developing general theories of victory for other threats, such as irregular and nuclear, the United States might face. An additional recommended area of future study is U.S. ability to deter adversaries from conducting hybrid war.

In order to efficiently and effectively develop a hybrid war theory of victory, the National Security, National Defense, and National Military Strategies must explicitly address hybrid war. This will serve to legitimize the concept and provide the motivation for many other study efforts. For this endeavor to be effective however, a commonly accepted understanding of the concept must be established. Currently, there are many different definitions and understandings of hybrid war, which only serve to confuse the debate.[118]

Additionally, further intellectual rigor in the cognitive domain must be expended on the hybrid war concept. This includes published and unpublished papers, journal articles, and books on the topic. Including hybrid war in secondary education curriculum is also warranted. Symposiums and conferences on hybrid war would be beneficial to expand the dialogue. From the "how to win" side of the equation, the United States Marine Corps appears to be a likely candidate to facilitate this type of activity. Various think tanks would be the logical choice to host events for thinking through the "what is winning" side of the theory of victory equation.

Another intellectual endeavor that would pay large dividends would be to establish an Advanced Studies Group (ASG) type school for senior elected and appointed national security decision makers and general officers. This school is intended to educate senior decision makers as the ASG schools intend to educate operational art experts. This would go a long way in

---

[118] In addition to the two definitions discussed in this paper, another example in a recent Joint Force Quarterly article is, "the simultaneous and intertwined application of conventional and irregular methods to achieve strategic objectives." Kenneth C. Coons Jr. and Glenn M. Harned, "Irregular Warfare is Warfare," *Joint Force Quarterly* (1st Quarter 2009), 103.

developing strategic coup d' oeil, similar in concept to Napoleon and Patton's operational level coup d' oeil. Bismarck would be an example worthy of emulation at such a school.

One problem with thinking about and developing a theory of victory is the lack of an explicit process or approach with which to frame it. Emerging concepts like "Design" in its many forms may have an application in designing a theory of victory. A design approach may enable an explicit description and explanation of what the problem actually is, what the desired state could and should "look like", what the theory of victory should be, and a strategy to achieve it. Approaches to problem framing and resolving such as design may help to achieve decisive strategic victory.

The United States' response to hybrid war will require it to meet complexity with complexity. This will require a whole of government approach that is very difficult for the United States to coordinate, plan, and deconflict. Much ink has been spilt of late with regards to improving inter-agency efforts; time will tell if any of these efforts prove fruitful.

Considering the perceived United States' military focus on the physical domain and its Jominian and Clausewitzian attitude towards defeating enemy forces, future adversaries' use of the cognitive and moral domains in hybrid war will challenge the United States. Strategic communication, public affairs, and information operations become critical and must be fully integrated for from the outset. They must be truly integrated into everything the military does and first, second, and third order effects of all actions must be considered. The use of information operations must be an overarching theme in any inter-agency approach in a hybrid war. The United States must improve its ability to fight in the cognitive and moral domains, or as Frank Hoffman espouses, "maneuver in the virtual dimension to achieve a positional advantage in the population's collective mind."[119] The notion of information operations supported by kinetic

---

[119] Frank G. Hoffman, "Conflict in the 21st Century: The Rise of Hybrid Wars," Potomac Institute for Policy Studies Monograph, Arlington, VA, December 2007, 53.

operations espoused by Colonel Darley is a concept with potential because, as earlier noted by Colonel Hammes, this is the way future adversaries will approach hybrid war.

It is possible the American strategic paradigm must reorient to give more emphasis to the cognitive and moral domains, just as potential enemies' paradigms have changed. It may be time to learn and adapt to the enemy's way of war with an increase in the effective use of the cognitive and moral domains. A good example is Hezbollah's use of the media in 2006 against Israel, described as a force multiplier to complement their asymmetric advantages.[120] Zawihiri's (al Qaeda's number two in command) comment that, "more than half of the Islamists' battle 'is taking place in the *battlefield* [emphasis added] of the media," is evidence of the importance current enemies place on the cognitive and moral domains.[121]

Lawrence Freedman, speaking of irregular warfare, a component of hybrid war, commented, "superiority in the physical environment is of little value unless it can be translated into an advantage in the information environment...Our enemies have skillfully adapted to fighting wars in today's media age, but for the most part we, our country, our government, has not."[122] It is evident that enemies of the United States have not just adapted to fighting in today's information age, they have defined fighting in today's information age.

Efforts must also be made to incorporate more constructive strategic guidance and interaction between political decision makers and senior military officers, especially operational level commanders. Better involvement by political leaders during military action and better involvement by military commanders during policy consideration that impacts military operations is necessary to ensure that war remains an extension of policy. There has typically been reticence

---

[120] Sarah E. Kreps, 80.

[121] Ibid.

[122] Col Doug King, USMC, "Hybrid War" (presentation to the Defense Science Board, 24 May 2007) quoted in Mackubin Thomas Owens, 70.

in both the U.S. political and military communities to mix the two spheres of influence, and for good reason. This demarcation, however, has led to a bifurcation of strategic thought that contributes greatly to an American way of battle vice an American way of war.[123]

Improving operational level doctrine would help develop a theory of victory as well. By incorporating the previously mentioned principles, doctrine would exist to guide operational level commanders and staffs in their campaign designs and planning of major operations with respect to a theory of victory. Current doctrine is exceedingly vague with respect to many critical concepts such as mission success criteria and conflict termination.[124] As Ikle' notes, "the question of terminating a war ought to arise as soon as the war has begun, or, indeed, in any advance planning."[125]

The U.S. military must spend additional energy at the operational and tactical levels of war as well.[126] TRADOC Pamphlet 525-5-500, *Commander's Appreciation and Campaign Design*, states that, "future violent conflicts are more likely to reflect what British General Rupert Smith has called 'war amongst the people.'"[127] It goes on to assert that even wars that begin as conventional state versus state conflicts, such as Operation Iraqi Freedom, are likely to involve aspects of irregular warfare.[128] While these documents address the challenges of internal,

---

[123] Antulio J. Echevarria, II, 7.

[124] U.S. Office of the Chairman of the Joint Chiefs of Staff, *Joint Operations*, Joint Publication (JP) 3-0 change 1, Washington, DC: CJCS, 17 September 2006 (Change 1, 13 February 2008), IV-5-IV-8 U.S. Office of the Chairman of the Joint Chiefs of Staff. *Joint Operation Planning*, Joint Publication (JP) 5-0, Washington, DC: CJCS, 26 December 2006, III-27.

[125] Fred Charles Ikle', 15-16.

[126] Another recommended area for future study is how operational art, or thinking operationally to translate strategic guidance into effective tactical tasks, as well as linking tactical outcomes to strategic success, is different in the context of a hybrid war.

[127] U.S. Army, *Commander's Appreciation and Campaign Design*, 4 and Rupert Smith, *The Utility of Force: The Art of War in the Modern World* (New York: Vintage Books, 2007), xiii.

[128] Ibid.

irregular warfare, they also describe many aspects of hybrid war as well. The military could make slight modifications to shift the focus to the hybrid war threat so that the ideas in these documents are applicable to an external threat.

The value of developing a hybrid war theory of victory, an evolving type of war, cannot be overstated. By undertaking these recommendations, a necessary mindset shift towards an American way of war will be accomplished. As Ikle' reminds us, "the purposes for which wars are fought can only be realized beyond the fighting."[129]

---

[129] Fred Charles Ikle', 14.

FIGURES

BIBLIOGRAPHY

abc.net, "U.S. admits to Suez Canal Killing," March 26, 2008.http://www.abc.net.au/news/stories/ 2008/03/26/2200141.htm (accessed September 23, 2008).

Advanced Research Projects Agency Social Science Department. Analysis of Vietnamization, A Description of the War, 1967-1971, May 1971.

Alberts, David S. and Richard E. Hayes. *Power to the Edge: Command and Control in the Information Age*. Washington D.C.: CCRP Publication Series, June 2003.

Alexander, John B. "The Changing Nature of War, the Factors Mediating Future Conflict, and Implications for SOF." Joint Special Operations University Report 06-01. Hurlburt Field, FL, April 2006.

American Heritage Dictionary. Second College Edition. Boston: Houghton Mifflin Company, 1985.

Arkin, William M. *Divining Victory: Airpower in the 2006 Israel-Hezbollah War*. Maxwell AFB, AL: Air University Press, 2007.

Axelrod, Robert and Michael D. Cohen. *Harnessing Complexity*. New York: Basic Books, 2000.

Bar-Yam, Yaneer. *Making Things Work: Solving Complex Problems in a Complex World*. Cambridge: Knowledge Press, 2004.

Bartholomees, J. Boone. "Theory of Victory." *Parameters* (Summer 2008): 25-36.

Benson, Kevin C.M. and Christopher B. Thrash. Declaring Victory: Planning Exit Strategies for Peace Operations. *Parameters* (Autumn 1996): 69-80.

Blank, Stephen J. "Georgia: The War Russia Lost." *Military Review* (November-December 2008): 39-46.

Bond, Brian. *The Pursuit of Victory: From Napoleon to Saddam Hussein*. New York: Oxford University Press, 1996.

Bond, Margaret S. "Hybrid War: A New Paradigm for Stability Operations in Failing States." U.S. Army War College Monograph, Carlisle Barracks, PA, March 2007.

Boot, Max. "Beyond the Three Bloc War." *Armed Forces Journal* (March 2006). http://www.armedforcesjournal.com/2006/03/1829753/ (accessed October 12, 2008).

————. *War Made New: Technology, Warfare, and the Course of History, 1500 to Today*. New York: Gotham Books, 2006.

Brafman, Ori and Rod A. Beckstrom. *The Spider and the Starfish: The Unstoppable Power of Leaderless Organizations*. New York: Portfolio, 2006.

Brown, Jeremy K., ed. *War in the 21st Century*. New York: H.W. Wilson Co., 2003.

Clausewitz, Carl von. *On War*. Edited and Translated by Michael Howard and Peter Paret. Princeton: Princeton University Press, 1976.

Coons, Kenneth C., Jr. and Glenn M. Harned. "Irregular Warfare is Warfare." *Joint Force Quarterly*. (1st Quarter, 2009): 97-103.

Coram, Robert. *Boyd: The Fighter Pilot Who Changed the Art of War*. New York: Little, Brown, and Co., 2002.

Carlo D'Este, *Decision in Normandy*. New York: E.P. Dutton, Inc., 1983.

Darley, William M. "Clausewitz's Theory of War and Information Operations." *Joint Forces Quarterly 40,* (1st Quarter 2006): 73-79.

Dunlap, Charles J. Jr.. "How We Lost the High-Tech War of 2007." *The Weekly Standard*. (January 29, 1996). http://www.weeklystandard.com/Content/Public/Articles/ 000/000/001/569nzbrd.asp (accessed 30 September 2008).

Echevarria, Antulio J. II, "Toward an American Way of War." U.S. Army War College Strategic Studies Institute Monograph, Carlisle Barracks, PA, March 2004.

Economist. "Grisly in Grozny." January 7, 1995.

Ellison, Sir Gerald. *The Perils of Amateur Strategy: As Exemplified by the Attack on the Dardanelles Fortress in 1915*. New York: Longmans, Green, and Co. Ltd., 1926.

Evans, Michael. "Australia and the Quest for the Knowledge Edge." *Joint Force Quarterly 30* (Spring 2002): 41-52.

————. "From the Long Peace to the Long War: Armed Conflict and Military Education and Training in the 21st Century," *Australian Defence College Occasional Series* (2007).

————. "History of Arms is the Difference." *United States Naval Institute Proceedings 124* (May 1998): 73-79.

————. "From Kadesh to Kandahar." *Naval War College Review* 56, no. 3 (Summer 2003): 132.

Flavin, William. "Planning for Conflict Termination and Post-Conflict Success." *Parameters* (Autumn 2003): 95-112.

Flournoy, Michele A. and Shawn Brimley, "The Defense Inheritance: Challenge and Choices for the Next Pentagon Team." *Washington Quarterly* (Autumn 2008): 59-76.

Freier, Nathan. "Strategic Competition and Resistance in the 21st Century: Irregular, Catastrophic, Traditional, and Hybrid Challenges in Context." U.S. Army War College Strategic Studies Institute Monograph, Carlisle Barracks, PA, May 2007.

Fuller, J.F.C. *The Foundation of the Science of War*. London: Hutchinson & Co., Ltd., 1925.

Galula, David. *Counterinsurgency War: Theory and Practice.* St Petersburg: Hailer Publishing, 1964.

Gat, Azar. *The Origins of Military Thought from the Enlightenment to Clausewitz.* Oxford: Clarendon Press, 1989.

Gates, Robert. Speech to the National Defense University, Washington, D.C., September 29, 2008.

Gray, Colin S., *Another Bloody Century: Future Warfare.* London: Weidenfeld and Nicholson, 2005.

———. "Defining and Achieving Decisive Victory." U.S. Army War College Strategic Studies Institute Monograph, Carlisle Barracks, PA, April 2002.

———. "Irregular Enemies and the Essence of Strategy: Can the American Way of War Adapt?" U.S. Army War College Strategic Studies Institute Monograph, Carlisle Barracks, PA, March 2006.

———. "Recognizing and Understanding Revolutionary Change in Warfare: The Sovereignty of Context." U.S. Army War College Strategic Studies Institute Monograph, Carlisle Barracks, February 2006.

———. *War, Peace, and International Relations. An Introduction to Strategic History.* New York: Routledge, 2007.

———. *War, Peace, and Victory: Strategy and Statecraft for the Next Century.* New York: Simon and Schuster, 1990.

Hammes, Thomas X. *The Sling and the Stone: On War in the 21st Century.* St Paul: Zenith Press, 2006.

———. "Fourth Generation Warfare Evolves, Fifth Emerges." *Military Review* (May-June 2007): 14-23.

Handel, Michael I. *Masters of War: Classical Strategic Thought, 3rd ed.* New York: Frank Cass Publishers, 2004.

Hanna, Elias. "Lessons Learned from the Recent War in Lebanon." *Military Review* (September-October 2007): 82-89.

Harper, David. "Targeting the American Will and Other Challenges for 4th-Generation Leadership." *Military Review* (March-April 2007): 94-104.

Hoffman, Frank G. "Conflict in the 21st Century: The Rise of Hybrid Wars." Potomac Institute for Policy Studies Monograph, Arlington, VA, December 2007.

———. "Hybrid Warfare and Challengers." *Joint Forces Quarterly.* (1st Quarter 2009): 34-48.

———. "The New Normalcy." *Foreign Policy Research Institute.* (May 12, 2006).

————. "4GW as a Model of Future Conflict." Address to the 2007 Boyd Conference, Quantico, VA, 13 July 2007.

Ikenberry, G. John. *After Victory: Institutions, Strategic Restraint, and the Rebuilding of Order After Major Wars.* Princeton: Princeton University Press, 2001.

Ikle', Fred Charles. *Every War Must End.* New York: Columbia University Press, 1991.

Joes, Anthony James. *America and Guerilla Warfare.* Lexington: University Press of Kentucky, 2000.

Jullien, Francois. *A Treatise on Efficacy.* Oahu: University of Hawaii Press, 2004.

Kalder, Mary. *New and Old Wars: Organized Violence in a Global Era.* Stanford: Stanford University Press, 1999.

Keegan, John. *A History of Warfare.* New York: Alfred A. Knopf Press, 1993.

Killibrew, Robert. "Good Advice: Hybrid Warfare Demands an Indirect Approach." *Armed Forces Journal* (June 2008). *http://www.armedforcesjournal.com/2008/06/3483224/* (accessed October 12, 2008).

Kober, Avi. "The Israel Defense Forces in the Second Lebanon War: Why the Poor Performance?" Department of Political Studies and BESA Center for Strategic Studies, Bar-Ilan University, Israel, February 2008.

Krause, Michael G. "Square Pegs for Round Holes: Current Approaches to Future Warfare and the Need to Adapt." *Land War Studies Center Working Paper No. 132,* Duntroon Australia, June 2007.

Kreps, Sarah E. "The 2006 Lebanon War: Lessons Learned." *Parameters* (Spring 2007): 72-84.

Kulikov, Sergey A. and Robert R. Love. "Insurgent Groups in Chechnya." *Military Review* (Nov/Dec 2003).

Liang, Qiao and Wang Xiangsui. *Unrestricted Warfare: China's Master Plan to Destroy America.* Panama City: Pan American Publishing Co., 2002.

Luman, Ronald R. ed. *Unrestricted Warfare Symposium.* Proceedings on Strategy, Analysis, and Technology. The Johns Hopkins University Applied Physics Laboratory, 20-21 March, 2007.

Mao, Zedong. *On Guerilla War,* 1937. http://www.marxists.org/reference/archive/ mao/works/1937/guerrilla-war/ (accessed January 29, 2009).

Mao, Zedong. *On Protracted War,* 1938. http://www.marxists.org/reference/archive/mao /selected-works/volume-2/mswv2_09.htm (accessed January 29, 2009).

Marks, Thomas A. "Insurgency in Nepal." U.S. Army War College Strategic Studies Institute, Monograph, Carlisle Barracks, PA, December 2003.

Martel, William C. *Victory in War: Foundations of Modern Military Policy.* New York: Cambridge University Press, 2007.

Mathews, Matt M. "We Were Caught Unprepared; The 2006 Hezbollah-Israeli War." *The Occasional Long War Series Paper 26.* U.S. Army Combined Arms Center Combat Studies Institute Press, Fort Leavenworth, KS, 2007.

Mattis, James N. and Frank G. Hoffman. "Future Warfare: The Rise of Hybrid Wars." *Proceedings Magazine 131* (November 2005) http://web.ebscohost.com.lumen.cgsccarl.com/ehost/detail?vid=4&bk=1&hid=117&sid=a2e0 4505-3278-4f6d-96ee-140cf1ba92fc%40sessionmgr102&bdata= JnNpdGU9ZWhvc3QtbGl2ZQ%3d%3d#db=mth&AN=18805095 (accessed October 12, 2008).

McCuen, John J. "Hybrid Wars." *Military Review* (March-April 2008): 107-113.

Michael, Kobi "The Dilemma Behind the Classical Dilemma of Civil-Military Relations: The "Discourse Space" Model and the Israeli Case During the Oslo Process," *Armed Forces and Society* 33, no 4, (July 2007).

Mintzberg, Henry. *The Rise and Fall of Strategic Planning: Reconceiving Roles for Planning, Plans, and Planners.* New York: The Free Press, 1994.

Mosier, John. *The Myth of the Great War: A New Military History of World War I.* New York: Harper Collins Publishers, 2001.

Nakhleh, Hany T. "The 2006 Israeli War on Lebanon: Analysis and Strategic Implications," United States Army War College Strategy Research Project, 2007.

Naveh, Shimon. *In Pursuit of Military Excellence: The Evolution of Operational Theory.* New York: Frank Cass, 1997.

Obama, Barak Hussein. "2009 National Defense Agenda." http://www.whitehouse.gov/ agenda/defense (accessed January 29, 2009).

Owens, Mackubin Thomas. "Reflections on Future War." *Naval War College Review 61,* (Summer 2008): 67-76.

Peters, Ralph. *Fighting for the Future: Will America Triumph?* Mechanicsburg: Stackpole Books, 1999.

Peters, Ralph. "Lessons from Lebanon: The New Model Terrorist Army." *Armed Forces Journal* (October, 2006). http://www.armedforcesjournal.com/2006/10/2069044/ (accessed January 18, 2009).

Pogue, Forest C. *George C. Marshall: Education of a General 1880-1939.* New York: Viking Press, 1963.

Record, Jeffrey. "Exit Strategy Delusions." *Parameters* (Winter 2001-02): 21-27.

Reed, James W. "Should Deterrence Fail: War Termination in Campaign Planning." *Parameters* (Summer 1993): 41-52.

Rittel, Horst W. J. and Melvin M. Webber. "Dilemmas in a General Theory of Planning." Paper presented to the Panel on Policy Sciences, American Association for the Advancement of Science, Boston, MA, December, 1969.

Rusling, Matthew. "Shifting Gears: For the military, a future of 'hybrid' wars." *National Defense.* (September 2008): 32-34.

Scales, Robert H., Jr. *Future War Anthology.* Carlisle Barracks: U.S. Army War College Press, 2000.

Schneider, James. "Carl von Clausewitz and Classical Military Paradigm." Briefing given to the School of Advanced Military Studies, Fort Leavenworth, KS, September 22, 2006.

Smith, Rupert. *The Utility of Force: The Art of War in the Modern World.* New York: Vintage Books, 2007.

Simpson, Erin M. "Thinking about Modern Conflict: Hybrid Wars, Strategy, and War Aims." Paper presented to the Annual Meeting of the Midwest Political Science Association, Chicago, IL, 7-11 April 2005.

Sorley, Lewis. *A Better War: The Unexamined Victories and Final Tragedy of America's Last Years in Vietnam.* New York: Harcourt, Inc., 1999.

Stewart, Del. "Deconstructing the Theory of 4th Generation Warfare." *Military Intelligence Professional Bulletin,* 2007.

Stroumpos, George. "A Concept for all Seasons." *Infantry Magazine,* 2007.

Sun Tzu. *The Art of War.* Translated by Samuel B. Griffith. New York: Oxford University Press, 1963.

Sun Tzu. *The Art of War.* Translated by J.H. Huang. New York: Quill, William Morrow Publishers, 1993.

U.S. Army. *Operations.* Field Manual (FM) 3-0 Washington, D.C.: Headquarters Department of the Army, 27 February 2008.

———. *Counterinsurgency.* Field Manual (FM) 3-24. Washington, D.C.: Headquarters Department of the Army, 15 December 2006.

———. *Commander's Appreciation and Campaign Design.* TRADOC Pamphlet 525-5-500. Fort Monroe, VA: Headquarters Department of the Army Training and Doctrine Command, 28 January 2008.

U.S. Department of Defense. *Irregular Warfare (IW) Joint Operating Concept (JOC),* Version 1.0, Washington, D.C.: 11 September 2007.

U.S. Department of Defense. National Defense Strategy. June 2008.

U.S. Marine Corps. *Hybrid Wafare and Challengers.* Strategic Vision Group Information Paper, 12 February 2008.

————. *SVG Strategic Trends and Implications.* Strategic Vision Group Information Paper, 12 February 2008.

U.S. Office of the Chairman of the Joint Chiefs of Staff. *Joint Operations*, Joint Publication (JP) 3-0 change 1, Washington, DC: CJCS, 17 September 2006 (Change 1, 13 February 2008).

————. *Joint Operation Planning*, Joint Publication (JP) 5-0, Washington, DC: CJCS, 26 December 2006.

Vlahos, Michael. "Fighting Identity: Why We Are Losing Our Wars." *Military Review* (November-December 2007): 2-12.

Von der Goltz, Freiherr. *The Conduct of War: A Short Treatise on its Most Important Branches and Guiding Rules.* London: Kegan Paul, Trench, Trubner and Co, Ltd, 1908.

Weigley, Russell F. *The American Way of War: A History of United States Military Strategy and Policy.* Bloomington: Indiana University Press, 1973.

CPSIA information can be obtained at www.ICGtesting.com
Printed in the USA
LVOW03s1156231015

459482LV00022B/1017/P